# Rewriting English

# THE NEW ACCENT SERIES

## General Editor: Terence Hawkes

*Alternative Shakespeares 1*, ed. John Drakakis
*Alternative Shakespeares 2*, ed. Terence Hawkes
*Post-Colonial Shakespeares*, ed. Ania Loomba and Martin Orkin
*Re-Reading English*, ed. Peter Widdowson
*Rewriting English*, Janet Batsleer, Tony Davies, R. O'Rourke, Chris Weedon
*English and Englishness*, B. Doyle
*Linguistics and the Novel*, Roger Fowler
*Language and Style*, E. L. Epstein
*The Semiotics of Theatre and Drama*, Keir Elam
*Structuralism and Semiotics*, Terence Hawkes
*Superstructuralism*, Richard Harland
*Deconstruction ed. 2*, Christopher Norris
*Formalism and Marxism*, Tony Bennett
*Critical Practice*, Catherine Belsey
*Dialogism*, Michael Holquist
*Dialogue and Difference: English for the Nineties*, ed. Peter Brooker/Peter Humm
*Literature, Politics and Theory*, ed. F. Barker, P. Hulme, M. Iversen, D. Loxley
*Popular Fictions: Essays in Literature and History*, ed. Peter Humm, Paul Stigant, Peter Widdowson
*Criticism in Society*, ed. Imre Salusinszky
*Fantasy*, Rosemary Jackson
*Science Fiction: Its Criticism and Teaching*, Patrick Parrinder
*Sexual Fiction*, Maurice Charney
*Narrative Fiction: Contemporary Poetics*, Shlomith Rimmon-Kenan
*Metafiction: The Theory and Practice of Self-Conscious Fiction*, Patricia Waugh
*Telling Stories: A Theoretical Analysis of Narrative Fiction*, Steven Cohan and Linda Shires
*Poetry as Discourse*, Anthony Easthope
*The Politics of Postmodernism*, Linda Hutcheon
*Subculture*, ed. 2, Dick Hebdige
*Reading Television*, John Fiske and John Hartley
*Orality and Literacy*, Walter J. Ong
*Adult Comics*, An Introduction, Roger Sabin
*The Unusable Past*, Russell J. Reising
*The Empire Writes Back*, Bill Ashcroft, Gareth Griffiths and Helen Tiffin
*Translation Studies* ed. 2, Susan Bassnett
*Studying British Cultures*, Susan Bassnett
*Literature and Propaganda*, A. P. Foulkes
*Reception Theory*, Robert C. Holub
*Psychoanalytic Criticism*, Elizabeth Wright
*The Return of the Reader*, Elizabeth Freund
*Sexual/Textual Politics*, Toril Moi
*Making a Difference*, ed. Gayle Green and Coppélia Kahn

AVAILABLE AS A COMPLETE SET: ISBN 0-415-29116-X

Janet **Batsleer**

Tony **Davies**

Rebecca **O'Rourke**

Chris **Weedon**

# Rewriting English

## Cultural Politics of Gender and Class

Routledge
Taylor & Francis Group
LONDON AND NEW YORK

First published 1985 by Routledge

This edition first published 2003
by Routledge
2 Park Square, Milton Park, Abingdon, Oxon, OX14 4RN

Simultaneously published in the USA and Canada
by Routledge

711 Third Avenue, New York, NY 10017

Routledge is an imprint of the Taylor & Francis Group

Transferred to Digital Printing 2007

First issued in paperback 2013



British Library Cataloguing in Publication Data
A catalogue record for this book is available from the British Library

Library of Congress Cataloging in Publication Data
A catalog record for this book has been requested

ISBN 978-0-415-29120-0 (hbk)
ISBN 978-0-415-85038-4 (pbk)

Publisher's Note
The publisher has gone to great lengths to ensure the quality of this reprint but points out that some imperfections in the original may be apparent

# Contents

*General editor's preface* vi
*Acknowledgements* viii

1 Culture and politics 1
2 Education: literacy and literature 13
3 Fiction as politics: working-class writing in the inter-war years 41
4 Gender and genre: men's stories 70
5 Gender and genre: women's stories 86
6 Remembering: feminism and the writing of women 106
7 Some women reading 140
8 Conclusion, in which nothing is concluded 155

*Notes* 176
*References* 179
*Index* 185

# General editor's preface

It is easy to see that we are living in a time of rapid and radical social change. It is much less easy to grasp the fact that such change will inevitably affect the nature of those disciplines that both reflect our society and help to shape it.

Yet this is nowhere more apparent than in the central field of what may, in general terms, be called literary studies. Here, among large numbers of students at all levels of education, the erosion of the assumptions and presuppositions that support the literary disciplines in their conventional form has proved fundamental. Modes and categories inherited from the past no longer seem to fit the reality experienced by a new generation.

*New Accents* is intended as a positive response to the initiative offered by such a situation. Each volume in the series will seek to encourage rather than resist the process of change; to stretch rather than reinforce the boundaries that currently define literature and its academic study.

Some important areas of interest immediately present themselves. In various parts of the world, new methods of analysis have been developed whose conclusions reveal the limitations of the Anglo-American outlook we inherit. New concepts of literary forms and modes have been proposed; new notions of the nature of literature itself and of how it communicates are current; new views of literature's role in relation to society flourish. *New Accents* will aim to expound and comment upon the most notable of these.

In the broad field of the study of human communication, more and more emphasis has been placed upon the nature and function of the new electronic media. *New Accents* will try to identify and discuss the challenge these offer to our traditional modes of critical response.

The same interest in communication suggests that the series should also concern itself with those wider anthropological and sociological areas of investigation which have begun to involve scrutiny of the nature of art itself and of its relation to our whole way of life. And this will ultimately require attention to be focused on some of those activities which in our society have hitherto been excluded from the prestigious realms of Culture. The disturbing realignment of values involved and the disconcerting nature of the pressures that work to bring it about both constitute areas that *New Accents* will seek to explore.

Finally, as its title suggests, one aspect of *New Accents* will be firmly located in contemporary approaches to language, and a continuing concern of the series will be to examine the extent to which relevant branches of linguistic studies can illuminate specific literary areas. The volumes with this particular interest with nevertheless presume no prior technical knowledge on the part of their readers, and will aim to rehearse the linguistics appropriate to the matter in hand, rather than to embark on general theoretical matters.

Each volume in the series will attempt an objective exposition of significant developments in its field up to the present as well as an account of its author's own views of the matter. Each will culminate in an informative bibliography as a guide to further study. And, while each will be primarily concerned with matters relevant to its own specific interests, we can hope that a kind of conversation will be heard to develop between them; one whose accents may perhaps suggest the distinctive discourse of the future.

TERENCE HAWKES

# Acknowledgements

Many people have contributed to the writing of this book, especially members of the English Studies Group at the Centre for Contemporary Cultural Studies between 1977 and 1980. We would like to thank Michael Denning, Brian Doyle, Hazel Carby, Tony Fry, Michael Green, Michael Lane, Michael Skovmand and Guillermo Sunkel. Special thanks are due to Roger Shannon, who made a considerable contribution to Chapter 4 on masculine romance, and to Myra Connell and Elaine Hobby for their work on women reading which forms an important part of Chapter 7. Janice Winship and Terry Hawkes have provided a good deal of constructive comment.

The authors and publisher are grateful to the following for permission to reproduce copyright material: For an untitled poem by Anne Bradstreet in Bernikow, Louise (ed.) (1979), *The World Split Open*. London: The Women's Press. UK and Commonwealth rights: The Women's Press; US rights: Louise Bernikow. For Household, Geoffrey (1968), *Rogue Male*. Harmondsworth: Penguin. UK and Commonwealth rights: Geoffrey Household and Michael Joseph Ltd; US rights: Little, Brown & Co. For Schools Council (1965) *Working Paper II*. London: HMSO. The Controller of Her Majesty's Stationery Office. For Spencer, J. (1971) *The English Language in West Africa*. London: Longman. J. Spencer and Longman Group Ltd.

# I
# Culture and politics

The idea of this book grew out of an investigation, by a group of students and lecturers at the Birmingham Centre for Contemporary Cultural Studies, into the literature of the 1930s. A simple enough matter, it might be thought, involving no doubt a good deal of reading, a sense of the historical context and pertinence of that reading, the rediscovery or revaluation of one or two neglected writers and a correspondingly revised estimate of some of the better-known ones. And as for the 'thirties', those years seemed, from the Wall Street crash to the Hitler–Stalin pact, from the death of D. H. Lawrence to George Orwell's 'Inside the Whale' and W. H. Auden's self-imposed exile, to define themselves with more than usual clarity as a 'decade', a distinct literary-historical period.

In the event, neither the 'literature' nor the 'thirties' – the two defining terms of that early project – turned out to be so obligingly uncomplicated. For one thing, we came rapidly to recognize that there were already a number of powerful versions of both in circulation. Their convergence around, and vested interest in, the literary pre-eminence of Orwell, Auden, Christopher Isherwood and Graham Greene, and in their various affiliations (for the thirties are, supposedly, the decade of 'commitment' . . .) and disaffiliations (. . . as well as of 'betrayal'), were of a kind to rule out any neutrally proffered additions or amendments. Those versions constituted not just one possible list among many of the 'major' writers of the decade, and of its significant political and historical issues and meanings, but a dominant grouping and a preferred narrative, whose force and value depend as much on what they exclude – the 'second-rate', the lowbrow, the popular – as on what they promote to the foreground. In this, we came to realize, they represent a kind of microcosm of the literary and literary-historical canon itself. For when we began to ask how that particular set of writers had been put together and promoted, in book after book, until it had become everybody's common sense about the period, we soon recognized that the 'thirties' themselves, far from being a simple topographical feature of the historical landscape, had similarly and often quite purposefully been *constructed*, at the time and later, as a significant entity, a shaped narrative – heroic or farcical or tragicomic – about what Orwell had called 'the invasion of literature by politics'.

That thirties project, then, set itself the task of compiling, around, behind and against the dominant versions, a more extensive and varied or simply more interesting account of the writing of the pre-war decade. Our aim was not to produce just another would-be 'definitive' reading of the period, but to problematize the very idea of literary periods and in particular to discern some of the forces and tendencies at work in a specific moment in what we came to call the 'literary formation'. This concept, by perhaps misleading analogy with the Althusserian notion of 'social formation', was intended to throw the emphasis away from anecdotal and descriptive accounts of writers and intellectual groupings and on to those relations of relative dominance and subordination, of centrality and marginality, of ideological difference and conflict, that characterize, the production and consumption of literature. By this time too the word 'literature' had become harder and harder to use unselfconsciously, since, with its hidden but powerful valuations and exclusions, it was itself clearly one of the forces structuring the historical and ideological ensemble we were attempting to analyse.

It should also be said that difficulties with the idea of 'literature', and a sense that any work that started there would be likely to remain imprisoned within the word's strong magnetic field, had another, more contingent source. This was the decidedly unsociable relations between cultural studies at the Birmingham Centre, where we were working, and literary criticism, which had, in the writings of Richard Hoggart and Raymond Williams, been one of its progenitors. By the mid-seventies, cultural studies retained few of the affiliations or concerns of Williams's *Culture and Society* or Hoggart's *Uses of Literacy*. In its much firmer engagement with Marxism and, rather differently, with feminism, it had turned to an interest in cultural manifestations and speculative developments that was not by any means hospitable to the idea of literature, as that word would be understood in a university English department.

For these reasons we determined to take our start not from 'literature' but from 'English studies': literary-critical ideologies and discourses, and their institutional locations and forms of power. We set out to treat these not as just another academic object of study requiring some anodyne historical sociology of literary tastes and attitudes, but as a problem and a challenge, calling for criticism and analysis of a sharper and more contestatory kind. Work of this sort is often described as 'contextual', and to the extent that it aims to break down the academic segregation and conceptual isolation of literature, the notion of 'context' is serviceable. But it can slide too easily into implicitly conceding the pre-eminence and assumed value of texts – not any old texts either, but *the* texts, the canon, the great tradition safely installed in the literature syllabus and regularly reconsecrated in the annual round of published criticism. The study of the thirties, though, had already taken us into areas and kinds of writing whose interest and significance lay far from any valuation of literary 'quality': to mass-market genres and 'middlebrow' novelists, to women's writing, to working-class fiction, as well as to a wider investigation of those institutions – such as schooling, publishing and broadcasting – whose active role in determining the meaning and value of writing and reading makes any treatment of them as inertly 'contextual' absurdly inadequate.[1]

These issues and problems have over the years remained central to our interests, and some of them are represented in the pages that follow. They are there in the critique of literature in education; in the account of the last great period, at least until the recent resurgence of worker-writer organizations, of working-class education and literature in the twenties and thirties; in the studies of popular literature, particularly as it is written and read by women; and in investigations of the new forms and practices of reading and writing associated with the women's liberation movement. At the same time, while the book (like the thirties project before it) moves beyond curricular literature and the discourses of English studies to consider practices of reading and writing that are largely excluded by the institutions of literary education and criticism, it also raises questions about those exclusions and those institutions which are likely to be central to any attempt to transform the study of English itself.

To the extent that the interests generated by the thirties project have developed and changed, they have also diverged. The following chapters, though historically grounded in themselves, range over a much wider period. In part this reflects a realization that forms of writing and practices of reading can properly be understood only in terms of their own relatively independent histories, and the uneven relations between them. But the move away from a more narrowly defined historical study is also prompted by an overriding concern for the cultural politics of the present moment, and by a conviction that the significance of history lies – though in no simply illustrative or exemplary way – in its importance for an understanding of the present.

The unity of the chapters that follow, then, is not of a conventional type. Each chapter is relatively discrete. Since they are no longer solely about the thirties, nor any longer concerned exclusively with the dominant discourse of English studies, their coherence now derives rather from a common politics, feminist and socialist, and from a shared form and habit of argument, both of which constitute an attempt to grasp the intricate and contradictory ways in which cultural processes and their products are inextricably enmeshed in the historical structures and power relations of class societies. This involves a recognition that, while images, narratives, meanings, the whole semiotic repertoire of a society, can never 'belong' in some absolute and unchanging sense to a single class, group or sex, slavishly encoding and reproducing their interests and values, neither can they, so long as they remain 'live' and active, escape what the Russian Marxist Vološinov, writing of language, called the 'multi-accentuality' of social conflict and inequality (Vološinov 1973, ch. 2). Thus even activities as apparently simple and fundamental as reading and writing are, in capitalist society, at one and the same time forms of regulation and exploitation *and* potential modes of resistance, celebration and solidarity. Every act of writing and reading, however apparently servile or mutinous, is marked by this double movement, echoing the cry of Caliban:

> You taught me language; and my profit on't
> Is, I know how to curse.

Our argument has tried to follow and enact this contradictory unity, leaning sometimes, in stressing the dominative aspects of capitalist patriarchy, to the critical mode; sometimes, in recording the persistent inventiveness with which people have resisted or evaded or appropriated its pressures, to the affirmative and celebratory. But generally, as in the exploration of mass-produced popular narratives, we attempt to hold a kind of contradictory median point, like those stories themselves, allowing a proper weight both to the potent representation of 'things as they are' and to the insurgent imagination of things as they might be.

We have called this a shared form of argument; and it is true that we have tried to find a way of writing that avoids as far as possible the twin temptations that beset cultural analysis on the left – moralistic denunciation and vacuous populist enthusiasm. But this is not really an intellectual or stylistic issue at all. It is a political one: how to acknowledge and comprehend the tremendous capacity of patriarchal and capitalist institutions to regenerate themselves not only in their material foundations and structures but in the hearts and minds of people, while never losing sight or despairing of the power of popular organization and struggle to resist and transform them. This represents an immediate and familiar dilemma for anyone who works (as in different ways all the authors of this book do) in the 'cultural apparatuses' of the state: education, community work, regional arts, and the like. In critical periods like the present, socialists and feminists in these institutions can find themselves seemingly defending the indefensible: not only their own comparatively privileged and sometimes quite powerful jobs, but entire institutions whose evident purpose and effect, thrown into even sharper relief by the imposed priorities of economic necessity and ideological discipline, is the reproduction of major forms of cultural privilege and social power. These ambiguities can be seen, for example, in higher education, where the benevolent paternalism of the 'Robbins principle' has given way to the unambiguous class interest of selective access and economic functionalism. This has obliged socialists to campaign for the restoration of a liberal ideology and practice of education with which they are likely to find themselves profoundly at variance, in a situation in which to argue strongly for socialist alternatives is likely to be seen as both divisive and futile. The fight over state funding for the arts, at a time when the argument is no longer about distribution and definition but about stark survival, offers another instance: what feminist or socialist would wish, in other circumstances, to defend the assumptions, the policies, the very existence of the Arts Council of Great Britain?

These contradictions and ambiguities, which are far more significant, interesting and painful than any supposed 'crisis in English studies', have emerged with increasing clarity and urgency over the period in which the book has been put together. They have compelled us to hope that it will be taken as a contribution, not, certainly, to literary criticism, nor even to cultural studies in the academic sense, but rather to a still undeveloped but possible and very necessary cultural politics of reading and writing. 'Cultural politics' is a concept, or rather a phrase, that has enjoyed a certain vogue in recent years, a vogue not always accompanied by any corresponding clarity of definition. Of course, what matters in the end is not whether cultural politics can be 'defined' (a question of lexicographic interest, at most), but whether it is a serviceable and productive notion, marking out an identifiable and feasible agenda of struggle, and suggesting ways of tackling it. But perhaps a brief consideration of the meanings of the phrase may throw some light on those questions too.

First, 'cultural politics' often seems to imply a contrast with some other kind of politics, usually 'real politics': that is, electoral and party politics, the politics of material need and provision, of insurrection and armed struggle, of the Politburo and the art of the possible. No priorities are necessarily implied, but in the dominant tradition cultural politics, if it has been recognized at all, has been firmly subordinated to the 'real thing'. This may be justified in the name of theoretical priority or of tactical necessity, or of both; rather in the manner of Brecht's sardonic phrase in *The Threepenny Opera*: 'grub first, ethics later'. In any case, it rests on a sharp conceptual division between politics and culture. This is often hard to sustain in the face of actual instances, and it certainly assumes a constricted and indeed conventional (i.e. bourgeois) notion of both culture and politics which the left might have been expected to challenge. None the less it remains characteristic of the Labour Party and the labour movement, as of British life in general, that it represents culture – even or especially in its narrow sense of books, theatre, music, entertainment – as having little or nothing to do with the serious business of politics and practical life. This separation is deeply rooted in the national mentality, and has had the result not only of depoliticizing culture but also, with equally impoverishing results, of 'deculturalizing' politics. Removing politics from the semiotic domain of signs, images and meanings, it segregates it from the lives and interests of 'ordinary people', who are in turn induced to accept the representation of themselves as incapable of, and bored by, political reflection and action.

A broader definition of culture, understood as a whole 'way of life' or 'way of struggle', with a consequent shift and expansion of the meaning of politics, has been a notable feature of 'New Left' thinking since the sixties. One example is provided by the libertarian and situationist initiatives of the later sixties, which actively refused both bourgeois and economistic Marxist definitions of politics and announced the irruption of culture, understood both as creativity and as a redeemed and unalienated everyday life, into the political domain. A more enduring and incalculably more significant instance has been the practical and theoretical challenge offered in recent years by the women's liberation movement. There too the traditional emphasis of male political activists on agendas, programmes and formalities of organization has been met by an insistence on the permanently and radically political character of everyday experience and private life, expressed in the phrase 'the personal is political'.

These differing senses of 'culture' and 'politics' ought not to be allowed to become programmatically absolute. It is worth remembering that, although the phrase 'cultural politics' is more likely to be encountered on the left, the dominant order, in its political institutions and state apparatuses, knows perfectly well what it means and why it matters. Indeed, the politics of symbols, subjectivities and meanings has proved an important component in the popular success of the new conservatism, with, for example, its use of spectacle as in the Falklands' War, its stress on individualism and authoritarianism and its redefinition of the enemy within. It may be that the cultural politics of the right will be making the running and defining the issues for the next few years at least. In these circumstances it will be as well to retain a degree of inventiveness and flexibility; indeed, it may even be necessary, on occasion, to leave 'culture' where it is and to concede the tactical (though never the absolute) priority of politics, old-style. (The authors of this book are, in fact, all active in politics, in this sense.) But it will always be important, too, to keep other senses, other grounds and resources of struggle, other imaginations of politics, alive and available.

Against this background, three broad areas of cultural-political practice might be outlined. In each, both culture and politics are given different contents and inflections, separately and together, suggesting the need not for some centralized 'programme' but for a great variety of different kinds of organization and strategy.

First, there is the struggle around the political and commercial organization of culture, in a fairly traditional sense: education, the arts, the sites and agencies of recreation and leisure.

Second, there is the issue of the cultural dimensions of politics: the language, symbolism and forms of representation of the political sphere. There are people on the left who cannot see a problem here and who believe that this has nothing to do with politics or vice versa. The cultural dimension of politics involves more than a mass-circulation labour movement tabloid. It must engage with its own sexism and racism, which among other things allow some activists to see nothing incongruous or problematic in urging British voters, more than half of them women, to 'ditch the bitch'.

Third, there is the battle over and for the political dimensions of culture, in its broadest sense. This is the most difficult as well as perhaps the most important area of cultural-political struggle. The difficulty is suggested by the fact that, with the important exception of the women's liberation movement, oppositional thinking about cultural politics, in this sense, has rarely advanced much beyond the hopeful incantation of a 'Gramscian' litany – hegemony, common sense, organic intellectuals, and the like.[2] Its practice, on the other hand, has been widespread in more or less disconnected and uncoordinated ways since the late sixties. It can be found in movements like 'Rock against Racism', in the anti-apartheid movement's interventions in and redefinitions of the politics of sport, in radical community and youth work, in the analysis of racism and political partisanship in seemingly neutral or innocuous things like television sitcoms and news bulletins. But all these, important and suggestive as they have been, have remained marginal to the labour movement, the Labour Party and the political consciousness of most people. They have been unable, thus far, to shift or extend the dominant meanings.

This is in part a problem of 'Englishness'. Those who re-experience their subjugation daily, at home, at work, in the street, know what cultural politics is, though few of them might call it that. Many Irish, Scots and Welsh know well enough that politics is a question of language, consciousness, identity, history. Black people understand that cultural struggle is no merely 'theoretical' issue. Women appreciate the hegemony of the pronoun and the politics of the joke. But the ruling culture of Englishness – white, male and (whatever its electoral habits) conservative – remains profoundly mistrustful of politics, as of culture, and resistant to its infiltration into everyday life. The disabling separation that makes 'cultural politics' such an intractable notion reflects the weakness and conservatism of our tradition, such as it is, of popular sovereignty. It reminds us that the British labour movement has never had to learn at first hand the terrible lessons of continental fascism: that capitalism is strong and cunning even in its moments of greatest weakness, and that its strength lies not only in its factories, armies and parliaments but in the rhythms and textures of culture, consciousness and everyday life.

This Englishness has left its mark on all of us. Non-English readers may feel at times, in the pages that follow, the constriction and airlessness of a certain parochialism, a preoccupation with figures and issues that seem, under a different sky, less momentous than we would make them. They should remind themselves that we are living out the dotage of an imperial culture, and that our dreams are peopled by ghosts. But from that culture we have inherited other habits too, towards which no indulgence can be extended; for the 'common politics' which, we have suggested, gives some kind of coherence to the cultural analyses and critiques that follow brings with it a uniformity of a more negative kind: its virtual blindness to questions of race. We have tried to keep in mind at every turn the interlocking relations of gender and class, but have failed to sustain any but the most transient and superficial recognition of a set of determinations every bit as basic and powerful, a structure of exploitation and a history of resistance of especially compelling relevance to political and cultural struggle in contemporary Britain. The book is, by that token, implicitly and actually *racist*, to the extent that it tacitly perpetuates and confirms the historical, cultural and political invisibility of black Britons. To call racism of this kind 'institutional' rather than intentionally willed may explain but can hardly redeem it. Capitalism and patriarchy are 'institutional', in this sense: pervasive, taken for granted, organic to the common sense of the dominant culture. If the book's aim is to contribute to the analysis and, thereby, to the transformation of the institutions of cultural power, it must also be acknowledged, as one of its many contradictions, that in this respect it speaks from and serves to reinforce those very institutions. If we invoke the curse of Caliban, we cannot prevent it falling on our own heads too.

These contradictions, ambiguities and absences, acknowledged and unacknowledged, define the ground of cultural struggle. This involves the re-accentuation of culture and the relocation of cultural practice within a collective social life. The scale, as well as the vagueness, of the project may serve as a reminder that it will take a long time and a long struggle before we can say that words like 'culture', 'politics', even 'literature', with their ingrained accents of possession, separation and exclusion, no longer have any interest and meaning for us.

An earlier volume in this series (Widdowson 1982) offered an influential and controversial analysis of the history and present predicament of English in higher education, and pointed to the existence, and the possible future development, of elements of an alternative practice. In expanding that analysis, and pursuing some of the suggested alternatives, the chapters that follow set out to define the politics of literacy and literature outside the institutions of literary criticism and of English in higher education. In a sense, this 'outside' must be understood to include much educational practice in schools; and it is with the politics of literacy and literature in schools, and its changing relationship with the literary institution, that we begin. The opening chapter traces some of the key historical shifts, against a background of cultural and social emergency, in the discourses of English in schools, and thus lays the groundwork for an understanding in a broader context of the issues raised in the rest of the book. The next chapter looks at working-class reading and writing in the crucial years between the wars, and, by suggesting some of the cultural and political circumstances determining the production of working-class writing, aims to throw some light on the problems of the material production and politics of writing which still face working-class, black and women writers operating outside the dominant institutions. We move next to a kind of writing whose relation to 'English' has always been at best ambivalent, more often antagonistic: formulaic popular fiction. Two chapters on 'gender and genre' attempt a reading, in close textual engagements as well as through the exploration of broader ideological themes, of the ways in which both masculine and feminine 'romances' help to constitute their readers' sense of gender and gender relations. Questions of gender are central to the next chapter, too, on the writing of women. Here we offer an account of some of the issues facing feminist writing, teaching and criticism at the present time, in particular the problems generated by conflicts between feminist political practice and the institutional powers of literary criticism, education and publishing. The chapter that follows, on women reading, while shorter and narrower in scope, asks what reading means to some working-class women whose reading habits have not been formed, at least directly, by a 'literary' education. The final chapter gathers many of these themes in a concluding reflection on the present cultural-political conjuncture in Britain. It points to the need to contest and transform the dominant cultural order both inside and outside the institutions of education, culture and politics, and draws on some of the discussion in earlier chapters to offer tentative thoughts on strategies for the future.

Finally, the collective authorship of this book should not be taken to imply a theoretical uniformity. It reflects shared political objectives and interests, while retaining considerable divergences of emphasis and approach. The 'we' of the text makes no pretensions to a unified collective subjectivity. Each chapter is the product both of individual reading and writing and of collective discussion. It is those many hours of discussion and argument among ourselves and with other people, over several years, that permit us to present what follows as a work of collective authorship and collective responsibility.

2

# Education: literacy and literature

My father was a working man
  and a collier was he,
at six in the morning they turned him down
  and they turned him up for tea.

My mother was a superior soul
  a superior soul was she,
cut out to play a superior role
  in the god-damn bourgeoisie.

We children were the in-betweens
  little non-descripts were we,
indoors we called each other *you*,
  outside, it was *tha* and *thee*.

(Lawrence 1929, pp. 82–3)

*Meryl.* If my mum heard me talking like that she'd bust my little ass. Your mum would as well?
*Audrey.* Yes, she'd say 'You're in England now, so talk English.' My dad's really got the Jamaican accent.
*Meryl.* If you were to say 'What a rass hole' and all this stuff at home would your mum start . . . my parents talk like that but when I do it they try and stop me.

(Federation of Worker Writers and Community Publishers 1978, p. 62)

In education, everyone is concerned about literacy. By no means everyone is concerned about literature. We're all expected to be literate. We're certainly not all expected to be 'literary'. Literacy is basic: people need it in order to do practically everything else. Literature isn't: most people get along quite nicely without it, most of the time.

There was a time when a literary education implied, among other things, very much what education in 'literacy' means now: the acquisition of the ability to read and write, the ability to do intelligible things with letters (*literae*). Since the eighteenth century, 'literature' has shrunk to its now severely contracted and specialized range of meanings, and 'literacy' has been recruited to cover some of the lost scope. But a narrowing has occurred within those meanings too. Eighteenth-century literacy, the preserve of a small propertied leisure class and its dependent intellectuals, meant a knowledge of Latin, certainly, and an easy familiarity with the poetry of Milton and Pope; but it also implied, within that narrow and privileged circle, a certain breadth and ease of personal expression. By the twentieth century, literacy has come more and more to denote things like spelling, punctuation, simple grammar – the elementary rules and rituals of a standardized official language called 'English'. It has tended to become, too, a narrowly educational matter, and the familiar anxieties about supposedly falling standards of reading, writing and spoken English reflect the growing institutional separation between the approved English of the classroom and the wide diversity of non-standard language outside.

There is a parallel here, to be taken up later. The native servants and petty functionaries of British India in the nineteenth century were patronized and ridiculed as 'babus' for the comic solemnity and officious would-be correctness of their English – a strain of racialist humour that survives in popular stereotypes of South Asian speech. But in Britain too, long before the empire started to 'come home' and the teaching of 'English as a second language' became a thriving educational enterprise, literacy has meant, for the majority of children in the majority of schools, the inculcation of a kind of indigenous 'babu' dialect, a 'second language' whose orthodoxies have little to do with the language of home or street. These children, contemporary equivalents of Lawrence's board-school 'in-betweens', are at the centre of current worries about literacy.

As for literature, few of those children, it may be supposed, will have much reason or occasion to concern themselves with *that*. The two words, literature and literacy, once so closely connected, have been separated by processes at whose centre lies an education system still fondly supposed to be dedicated to 'equality of opportunity'. These processes are long and complex, and engage some of the deep historical themes of contemporary British society.

## Literature and mass society: what Maisie didn't know

Writing in the closing days of the nineteenth century, the novelist Henry James turned his thoughts to the 'future of the novel' and found the prospect 'of a sort to engender many kinds of uneasiness'. He noted, first, the sheer and unparallelled profusion of print, and of popular fiction in particular:

> The book, in the Anglo-Saxon world, is almost everywhere, and it is in the form of the voluminous prose fable that we see it penetrate easiest and farthest.
>
> (James 1899, p. xi)

This abundant increase in the volume of publication he related to changes in the size and social composition of the 'reading public'.

> There is an immense public, if public be the name, inarticulate, but abysmally absorbent, for which, at its hours of ease, the printed volume has no other association [than 'mere mass and bulk']. This public, the public that subscribes, borrows, lends, that picks up in one way and another, sometimes even by purchase – grows and grows each year, and nothing is thus more apparent than that of all the recruits it brings to the book the most numerous by far are those that it brings to the 'story'.
>
> (James 1899, pp. xi–xii)

Like most literary intellectuals, then and since, James viewed these developments with alarm. 'The flood at present swells and swells, threatening the whole field of letters . . . with submersion' (p. xii). So far the sentiments are familiar, even banal. 'Things fall apart' is the conventional refrain of the *literati* since at least the eighteenth century. From Pope's comminations in *The Dunciad* against the impending inundations of 'Dulness' and Grub Street to the querulous anxieties of every second Sunday reviewer, writers of a certain sort have claimed to be defending the 'field of letters' – the values and privileges of bourgeois literary culture – against a supposedly engulfing tide of popular commercial trash. But James's account of the character and tastes of the expanding fiction-reading public is more interesting and particular than this, for he relates them directly to the educational institution of mass literacy, and of *female* literacy in particular.

> The diffusion of the rudiments, the multiplication of common schools, has had more and more the effect of making readers of women and of the very young. . . . The larger part of the great multitude that sustains the teller and the publisher of tales is constituted by boys and girls; by girls in especial, if we apply this term to the later stages of the life of the innumerable women who, under modern arrangements, increasingly fail to marry – fail, apparently, even, largely, to desire to.
>
> (James 1899, p. xii)

This last remark suggests that, for the author of *The Bostonians*, the typical popular reader is not only female but also, tendentially, feminist. But, feminist or not, the female reader, and indeed the female writer, is presented as irredeemably 'inarticulate', 'absorbent', generically incapable of those feats of sustained formal organization that characterize, in its production and its reception alike, the authentic 'art of fiction'. In an earlier essay on Flaubert, he had earlier contrasted the poised and conscious craft of the (male) novelist with the fictional effusions of 'a sex ever gracefully, comfortably, enviably unconscious (it would be too much even to call them suspicious) of the requirements of form'. And here he associates that formal and critical incapacity directly with the imminent general collapse of literary and cultural standards and values:

> The high prosperity of fiction has marched, very directly, with another 'sign of the times', the demoralization, the vulgarization of literature in general, the increasing familiarity of all such methods of communication, the making itself supremely felt, as it were, of the presence of the ladies and

> children – by whom I mean, in other words, the reader irreflective and uncritical.
>
> (James 1899, p. xiv)

It would be easy, and quite inadequate, to dismiss these sentiments as a historical oddity, as mere polemic for a privileged male élite – though they *are* both. For one thing, they touch, in characteristically teasing and ironic fashion, on a cluster of themes – literary culture, mass literacy, feminism, popular fiction – which are central too, in their later historical extensions and intrications, to our arguments in this book. And just as James's fiction stands in a seminal relation to Anglo-American literary modernism, so this essay can be seen as one of the founding documents of the professional practice of 'literary criticism'. Its arguments, and just as importantly its *mood*, flow quite directly, for example, into Q. D. Leavis's very influential *Fiction and the Reading Public* (1932), and thence into *Scrutiny* and its later diffusions. Its insistence on the formal rigour and self-consciousness required of novelist and reader alike, against the background of a threatened literary culture, informs both F. R. Leavis's demand for moral and intellectual 'intensity' (a key word for James too) and John Crowe Ransom's very differently inflected prospectus for the professionalization of literary criticism:

> Rather than occasional criticism by amateurs, I should think the whole enterprise might be seriously taken in hand by professionals. Perhaps I use a distasteful figure, but I have the idea that what we need is Criticism, Inc., or Criticism, Ltd.
>
> (Ransom 1968, p. 329)

F. R. Leavis, who undoubtedly *would* have found that figure distasteful (sharing with James a pre-capitalist, artisanal conception of the writer's and critic's 'craft'), installed James among the 'classical critics'. This was for his defence of the novel (as opposed, sharply, to mere 'fiction') as an art form and for his insistence that 'for the critic and the "educated" reader to be ignorant of their corresponding obligation was ignoble'. More recent examples could be multiplied. Wayne Booth's *Rhetoric of Fiction* (1961), for instance – a book that has done a good deal in its turn to inform the practice of a later generation of stockholders in Criticism, Inc. – is saturated in Jamesian assumptions: it is, indeed, an extended reflection on his practice as novelist and critic.

This is sketchy, of course, and could be much amplified. But a pattern of recurrent oppositions is already beginning to emerge. On one side, literature, the 'art of fiction', with its attendant spirit, 'criticism'; on the other, mass literacy, popular fiction, and the sort of reading that James characterized as 'an obscure, confused, immediate instinct' (James 1899, p. xii). The first belongs to the writer's atelier, the metropolitan review and, increasingly, as the new century wears on, to the university. The second evokes (to quote James again) 'the flare of railway bookstalls, the shopfronts of most booksellers, especially the provincial, the advertisements of the weekly newspapers'. And that broad and familiar picture of cultural opposition and 'decline' subtends other categorial oppositions: of class and, as importantly, of gender. The professional and 'educated' reader, writer and critic is seen, generically, as bourgeois, metropolitan and male; the popular writer and reader as lower-class, provincial and female. In this process the corresponding general qualities – intelligence against instinct, organization against formlessness, professional against amateur – become classed and gendered too.

There is nothing in the least surprising about all this. Of course the cultural power of capitalist societies was and remains bourgeois and male. It could hardly be otherwise, though the phrase 'cultural power' quite fails to express the complex and internally contradictory character of a highly developed social formation. The plangent and uncertain tone of James's essay may be taken as indicative of the sharp anxiety induced, in intellectuals uneasily aware of the true basis and nature of their 'civilization', by the ominous proximity of what Tennyson in *Locksley Hall* had called 'a hungry people . . . creeping nigher . . . behind a slowly-dying fire': not only the urban working class, but the women's movement, the organization of labour, the often unconcealed brutality and venality of domestic and imperial politics alike.

But the point is this: that the institution of elementary state education – of 'literacy' – and of the university discipline of English – of 'literature' – occur across a half-century of deep and varied social crisis, in the course of which the dominant modes of social and sexual authority are repeatedly called into question. The response of the British ruling class to this challenge was not confined, needless to say, to the inauguration of Schools of English Literature at Oxford (1893) and at Cambridge (1917), nor even to the obligatory consignment to memory in a thousand elementary schools of large and edifying portions of Palgrave's *Golden Treasury* (1861). But the institutions of cultural and linguistic hegemony, and the ideological struggles that they articulate, are no less 'material' than guns and prisons. From the years of the Paris Commune to those of the October revolution, a chorus of public voices in England amplified the Jamesian concerns; and those concerns converged increasingly on the education system as the institution most likely to contain, manage and resolve the crisis by giving it a cultural-linguistic form.

## Literature, nation and empire

> We state what appears to us to be an incontrovertible primary fact, that for English children no form of knowledge can take precedence of a knowledge of English, no form of literature can take precedence of English literature: and that the two are so inextricably connected as to form the only basis possible for a national education.
>
> (Newbolt 1921, p. 14)

It is important, if its subsequent history is to make sense, to recognize that state education in England has been from the outset not 'classical' or historical or scientific or technical, but *literary*. This is not to say that all those subjects and others did not find a place in the curriculum of state schools, though Latin and Greek remained almost exclusively the preserve of private ('public') and grammar schools and of the ancient universities. But the centre of the curriculum – though for the majority of children, as we shall see, an absent centre – the point from which all the rest flowed and on which it depended for its coherence, was occupied by English language and literature.

Reasons for this are complex; but among them must be counted the unusual pre-eminence accorded to literature by the liberal intellectual culture within which the ultimately dominant conceptions of universal state schooling were elaborated. For Matthew Arnold the 'culture' to which we must look to redeem the inevitable 'anarchy' of class interest was, virtually, the national literature. For his contemporary John Stuart Mill, literature alone could animate the shallow utilitarian materialism of nineteenth-century intellectual and practical life. For Henry Sidgwick, 'liberal education' opposed the humane breadth and warmth of poetry to the narrower claims of science and classical scholarship.[3] And, if language and literature were indeed, as Newbolt claimed, 'inextricably connected', then the language of literacy must be language of literature. Not, to be sure, the language of Falstaff or Mrs Gamp, but the purified, idealized, standardized essence of literary language: 'systematic training in the use of standard English, to secure clearness and correctness both in oral expression and in writing' (Newbolt 1921, p. 19).

There is a substantial conformity here, across more than half a century. From Arnold to Newbolt, literature matters because of its indispensable relation to an evolving ideology of public education. And education matters, supremely, because more than anything else, more than the vote, the popular press, the management of political opinion, it must win the consent of those classes and groups dispossessed and subordinated by capital, and weld it, as capital vastly expands its field of exploitation, to a common conception of imperial nationhood. Here, as ever, the Newbolt Report is admirably explicit and succinct:

> In France, we are told, this pride in the national language is strong and universal. . . . Such a feeling for our own native language would be a bond of union between classes, and would beget the right kind of national pride. Even more certainly should pride and joy in the national literature serve as such a bond.
>
> (Newbolt 1921, p. 22)

It should be clear that this is not a question of 'bias' or 'indoctrination', of 'capitalist schooling' in some crudely mechanical sense. Schools did, of course, contribute directly to the expansive imperialist hegemony of those years. Many thousands of working-class children learnt their letters from *The*

*Boys' Book of British Heroes* or *Daughters of the Empire*, and were encouraged thus to think of themselves, in ways often directly racist, not as the subordinate *class* of a capitalist society but as the ruling *nation* of a great empire. *Akenfield*, for example, records a typical Empire Day celebration in rural Suffolk in 1907 in which 'her Ladyship kindly lent 20 flags and the children were taught to salute the Union Jack. Lessons were given on the Union Jack and "the Growth and Extent of the British Empire". Several patriotic songs were sung' (Blythe 1972, p. 169). Such overt manipulations are not trivial, and continue to provide occasions of immediate and necessary struggle within the curriculum.

But much more fundamental, and certainly much harder to resist or even to detect, are the ways in which the whole curriculum itself, along with the entire regime and official culture of the school, silently and objectively institutionalizes the dominant order. It is at this level, rather than in any browbeating Gradgrindery in the classroom, that language and literature, in their distinctive unity, came to serve the hegemonic purposes of British education. As many generations of painful and confusing experience now testify, to become 'literate', and still more – for a few – to come to acknowledge the value of 'literature', is, for a working-class child, to be caught up in a social and ideological process that is profoundly ambiguous and disorienting in its movement and destination. If that experience has become, over the past century, part of the familiar folklore of the white working class, black children have recently, and much more sharply, begun to rediscover it in all its rawness and contradiction.

The installation of literature, or rather of language-through-literature, as 'the only basis possible for a national education' did not come about without an argument. Through the formative 1860s, for example, the counter-claims of natural science were vigorously pressed. Against Arnold, Thomas Huxley maintained that 'for the purpose of attaining real culture, an exclusively scientific education is at least as effectual as an exclusively literary education' (Mathieson 1975, p. 25). Half a century later, with what Kipling called the 'salutary lesson' of the Boer War fresh in the memory of politicians and educators, the achievements of the Prussian high school and technical college were frequently offered as evidence of the superiority for a warlike and imperial power of a scientific and technical curriculum. But, although the technical high schools of the 1944 Act, like the technical colleges and polytechnics of the post-war period, testify to the persistence in secondary and tertiary education of these different conceptions, and though Latin and Greek maintained for a long time their hegemony in the curricular formation of ruling-class intellectuals, the education of the great majority of working-class and middle-class children was dominated and infiltrated, from the 1880s on, by the prestige and authority of the national literature.

That literature was from the outset selected and constructed in terms of the ideological purposes of a particular educational practice.

> Literature consists of all the books – and they are not so many – where moral truth and human passion are touched with a certain largeness, sanity and attraction of form. . . . This is what makes literature, rightly sifted and rightly studied, not the mere elegant trifling that it is so often and so erroneously supposed to be, but a proper instrument for a systematic training of the imagination and sympathies, and of a genial and varied moral sensibility.
>
> (Palmer 1965, pp. 93–4)

This quotation from the liberal politician John Morley in 1887 exhibits instructively the distinctive combination of elevated moral tone and conscious instrumentality that characterizes many subsequent definitions of literature, including Newbolt's and, we may say, Leavis's. But beneath the lofty thoughts, the noble sentiments and the great inspiring universals runs a different and more urgent refrain: Robert Lowe's 'we must educate our masters',[4] or George Sampson's 'Deny to working-class children any common share in the immaterial, and presently they will grow into men who demand with menaces a communism of the material' (Sampson 1925, Preface). Literature and revolution, wrote Trotsky. Literature *or* revolution, warned Newbolt, Sampson, even Leavis. For in a declarative editorial ('Under which king, Bezonian?') Leavis mapped out the *Scrutiny* project in terms of its polar opposition to Marxism.[5] These are the imperatives that underpin the 'disinterested' evaluations and discriminations of the 'great tradition', both for those who will study and then teach it, and for those less 'fortunate' or 'gifted' who will encounter it only in the displaced and neutral form of educational standard English.

The period of this major settlement runs in England from, say, 1860 to 1930. The whole repertoire had already been rehearsed, however, almost a century before the liberal education debate in England, in the establishment of a curriculum for the imperial dominions. For 'English literature' was born, as a school and college subject, not in England but in the mission schools and training colleges of Africa and India. There too the primary emphasis falls, at the outset, on linguistic standardization and conformity. The Freetown community in Sierra Leone, for example, was established in 1791. 'In the missionary schools of Freetown and in the churches, what one might call "establishment English" was used. No longer the brutal commercial exchanges of the slavers; the "civilizing mission" of Europe had begun' (Spencer 1971, p. 13). But the medium and standard of linguistic hegemony becomes, quite early on, literature. The 1835 'Macaulay memorandum' on Indian education recommended 'imparting to the native population a knowledge of English literature and science through the medium of the English language' (Press 1963, p. 14). A minute of 1867 from the Ceylon Committee brings out succinctly both the hegemonic character of the national language and literature and the function they were soon to assume for the subaltern population of the imperial metropolis, where the education of the ruling class was still securely classical: 'English should be to the natives of Ceylon what Latin is to the natives of Great Britain' (Press 1963, p. 14*n.*) – a comparison already drawn twenty years earlier, in Africa, by the Scots mission teacher Hope Waddell:

> By the aid of missionaries and schools [English] may be made the common medium of communication, yea, the literary and learned language of all Negro tribes as the Roman language was to the modern nations of Europe while yet the modern European languages were in an infantine and unwritten state.
>
> (Spencer 1971, p. 14)

A historian of education in the subcontinent, G. E. Perren, has remarked, of a period a full century before Newbolt, Richards and Leavis, that 'the whole concept of "English education" in India was intimately bound up with an expressed belief in the value of English literature' (Press 1963, p. 14); and this has continued to be the case, as Empire declined into Commonwealth, in the major neo-colonial dependencies. Another writer notes of contemporary West Africa that

> if we look at the school syllabus, past or present, we get one kind of answer. Schools have been teaching the English of the textbooks, of Wordsworth, Shelley and Tennyson, of *The Mill on the Floss* or of *Black Beauty*.
>
> (Spencer 1971, p. 4)

The English Department in the University of Khartoum is advertised, approvingly, as 'a main channel for the cultural influence of Western thought, literature and arts' (Spencer 1963, p. 93), and a Leverhulme working party advises African universities and colleges that

> throughout all the literature courses . . . attention should be paid to the literary language. This can be admirably done through such techniques as textual analysis (e.g. along the lines of the French *explication de texte* or the English modified Practical Criticism).
>
> (Spencer 1963, p. 125)

True, this literary-linguistic imperialism has in recent years assumed the humbler and more ingratiating tones appropriate to a neo-colonialism of 'influence', 'aid' and 'development'. Nowadays it will remind us with modest pride of 'the modernizing influence that a study of English literature has exercised overseas', or suggest coyly that 'Britain has more than a means of communication to give the world . . . she has through her literature her own personal contribution to make' (Press 1963, p. 84). But the infrastructure of cultural-linguistic domination persists, often in surprisingly crude and mechanical forms. As early as 1937 an official report on higher education in East Africa was protesting that

> in secondary schools in Great Britain, the hours devoted to English are frequently taken up by teaching, not the English

> language, but English literature. This practice tends to be transplanted from the home country into African schools, where conditions do not justify it.
>
> (Press 1963, p. 16)

Thirty years later, another observer complained that in Ghana

> a disproportionate amount of time is spent in teaching the section of the syllabus concerned with English literature, and which requires candidates to read . . . authors like Shakespeare, Milton, Wordsworth, Keats and Jane Austen.
>
> (Spencer 1971, p. 62)

Even today, in spite of these misgivings, the universities of Cambridge and London, operating through the Overseas School Certificate and the General Certificate of Education, and backed by the institutional prestige of the British Council and the commercial power of educational publishing, continue to give concrete and very profitable force throughout Africa and the Far and Middle East to that conception of standard English memorably expressed in 1862 by a mission teacher in Africa: 'a language which seems of itself to raise the person who is acquainted with it to the scale of civilization' (Spencer 1971, p. 13).

This is not the usual history of 'English'. But it may serve, at the very least, as a useful corrective background against which the familiar account may be seen more clearly. For the two narratives, the development of a 'humanist discipline' at home and the story of its more directly and often nakedly dominative uses overseas are, as the Newbolt Report might say, inextricably connected, and help richly to illumine one another.

## Learning to discriminate

> I remember some years ago when discussing the modern situation with the late Professor Karl Mannheim and Dr Lowe, I listened to what they said about the importance for us here of Philosophy, and the acquisition through it of a common *Weltanschauung*. My wife interrupted to say: 'We English, unlike you Germans, do not get our *Weltanschauung* through Philosophy, but through Poetry.' I am sure that is true. I am sure that in English Poetry we have an inestimable

> cultural treasure which we neglect at our cost, and that our hope of retaining a firm sense of spiritual values depends on our being taught when young to love and treasure our great inheritance of English poetry.
>
> (Lord Lindsay, in Wrenn and Bullough 1951, p. 168)

Literature, as a concept and a practice, is a particular selection and organization of texts ('rightly sifted and rightly studied'), defined principally by its position and function in the curricular and pedagogic economy. So much might be widely conceded nowadays. The recognition of the selectiveness and historical determinacy of literary traditions has been called by Raymond Williams a 'crucial theoretical break' (Williams 1977, p. 53). But theoretical breaks have a way of remaining harmlessly theoretical, and this one, as Carole Snee has observed, 'is itself in danger of being incorporated into the dominant cultural tradition rather than being used to challenge it' (Clark 1979, p. 166). The situation is familiar. On one side, a whole series of 'radical' approaches has been, a few Lancastrian and Cantabrigian hiccups apart, smoothly accommodated and immobilized by the liberal pluralism of the literary-academic apparatus.[6] No publisher's list or undergraduate course on 'varieties of criticism' is complete without its house-trained specimen of Marxism, feminism, post-structuralism or the sociology of culture. All too often, indeed, and with the best of intentions, these have by their Byzantine complexity and difficulty actually reinforced the bewilderment and tedium that already alienate most students and ordinary readers from the subject. On the other hand, much of the genuinely oppositional writing that has, in Terry Eagleton's phrase, 'discourteously refused' to take its place in the family photo has been simplistic and thus easily dismissed: windy affirmations of 'them and us' in literature.

From the point of view of the dominant practice, the result is much the same in both cases. The well-behaved pluralist joins the club, and subscribes to the rules. The tough-talking activist doesn't get past the bouncer, and can safely be ignored. There's no point in talking about 'failures' here, but the predicament ought to alert us to the formidable resilience and durability of literary institutions and of the ideologies that animate them. Two aspects of this are worth emphasizing: the extent to which literary ideologies have been able to exercise an unchallenged monopoly of the means of discursive legitimacy within their own very extensive orbit, and their remarkable capacity to absorb, transform and neutralize political impulsions, including their own. The first of these means that any account of those texts and traditions constituted as 'literary', and thus as the proper object of literary criticism, must either establish its credentials in terms legitimated by the literary discourse as a whole – the entire field of statements and assumptions about the subject, explicit or implicit – and so concede itself as a variety of mainstream criticism, or else risk being dismissed without further ado as an unwanted interloper (from psychology or sociology or philosophy or history or simple impertinence).

There is nothing sinister about this process, whereby statements, questions and objects of enquiry are sorted and placed in terms of underlying and usually unstated criteria of relevance. It is a feature of all discursive activities, and fundamental to the intellectual culture of class societies. But its particular importance here lies in the especially strong and central position occupied in that culture by literary discourse, a position that enables it to displace and supplant historical, social and, above all, political analysis of cultural activity as too narrow, parochial and partisan and to offer itself as a 'totalizing' explanation, ecumenical, disinterested and classless. Here, the effective absence in England of a formally constituted academy and of a correspondingly organized and self-conscious literary clerisy, though deplored by Arnold, has proved in the event a valuable asset to the cause he promoted. It has enabled the discourses of literature to deflect theoretical challenge and embarrassment by appealing to a tradition of sturdy British common sense and empirical knowledge, and has rendered them uncommonly resistant to systematic argument and refutation. If a historian offers the opinion that, say, the Treaty of Versailles is the most significant event in modern European history, we feel justified in expecting some supporting argument, in detail and fundamentals. But, when a literary critic intimates that *The Fat Boy of the Fifth* is, self-evidently, the most important English novel of the century, it is by no means clear what exactly is being asserted, or to what purpose. Notoriously, supporting argument is likely to consist of little more than a stately round-dance of self-corroborating terms ('richness'? 'immediacy'? 'felt life'?) whose major virtue lies in their being incapable of demonstration or even definition. Any evidence for the judgement is likely to be drawn entirely from the text whose superiority is being asserted in the first place, with at best a glancing dismissal of some other text selected for the purpose of being asserted to be inferior. To demur, or rather to make the next move in the game, in the genial, senior-common-room mode no less than in the impassioned oppositional rhetoric of the Scrutineer, it is necessary only to repeat the process, but with *Biggles Flies East* instead. Hence the celebrated 'consensus' of liberal criticism: 'This is so, isn't it?'

All this may look harmless enough. But what is 'so' is, commonly, a matter of 'discrimination' – that is, of invidious comparison. Take a celebrated example of discriminative 'placing': 'We shall not find Swift remarkable for intelligence if we think of Blake' (Leavis 1952, p. 87). How do two writers so strikingly different, divided historically by the best part of a century, and offering, one would think, so few points of promising comparison, come to find themselves bedded down together in the same discriminating sentence? Or again: Fielding 'is important not because he leads to Mr J. B. Priestley but because he leads to Jane Austen, to appreciate whose distinction is to feel that life isn't long enough to permit of one's giving much time to Fielding or any to Mr Priestley' (Leavis 1948, p. 11).

Statements of this kind – and, apart from the bullying tone, they are generally representative – are both tendentious and arbitrary: arbitrary because apparently substantive terms are in fact reversible and replaceable (try switching Swift and Blake round, or substituting Mickey Mouse and Donald Duck, and see if it makes any difference), tendentious because acceptance of the central values ('intelligence', 'distinction') implies assent to an unstated argument which in its turn derives its force from the assumed acceptance of those values – a perfect circularity. Needless to say, this academic terrorism actively and deliberately precludes any consideration of social, historical or political circumstances and positions. The Swift–Blake comparison is a good example of this. Not only are the two writers treated as though they were contemporaries and social equals; the comparison ruthlessly ignores the successive political urgencies –

the party racket, colonialism and landlordism in Ireland, religious conformity and dissent, the American and French revolutions – and the utterly different formal options, in the absence of which the contrasting radicalisms of Blake and Swift are reduced to vacuous trivialities about 'intelligence'. And all this in the name of a critical practice that boasts of its concreteness, its distaste for mere generalities.

The key terms of liberal criticism – intelligence, distinction, discrimination, evaluation, judgement – are rigorously purified, drained of all social and historical content. If we permit some of their other meanings and contexts to creep back in, however, it becomes possible to see literary criticism as a discourse and a practice in which certain words with a very powerful charge of social meaning are doing something other than they appear to be. From this point of view, literary canons appear not just as selections but as hierarchies, whose value derives not from any intrinsic properties but from the fact that they necessitate a continuous process of comparative placing and opposition. It does not matter at all, in any absolute sense (though it may matter individually to one person or another), whether Donne is a 'better' poet than Milton, or Conrad a 'greater' novelist than Hardy. But it matters very much for the effective functioning of literary ideologies and their practical outcomes – GCE results, degree classifications, careers in the academy – that writers and texts should continue to be opposed to one another in this fashion. Of course, readers will always prefer some texts and writers to others, for perfectly legitimate reasons that we may call 'personal' or 'subjective' but that are in their actual origin historical, social, sexual, familial, in all their immense mutual complexity. Most readers have always recognized this. But literary criticism confers on this quite normal activity something of the intensity, exclusiveness and intolerance of a religious sect. It lifts it out of the everyday circumstances of reading and conversation and claims for it, in the name of some shibboleth such as 'beauty', 'significance' or – absurdly – 'life', the status of a transcendent ethical value.

This apprenticeship in discrimination is, of course, reserved for a minority, in the universities and the literary and literary-critical professions. It is, we might say, itself a practice of discrimination, in a broader sense, standing as it does at the end of a long process of selective preparation and evaluation. Primary-school children are not, formally, required to debate the respective merits of *Billy Blue-Hat* and *Janet and John Go Shopping*. Even at GCE Advanced level, the selection of texts, and the underlying canon, with Chaucer, Shakespeare and Milton as near-invariables, some modern poetry or fiction for 'relevance', and so on, are substantially given. The examination papers do not – decidedly – encourage any exercise of evaluative enterprise or innovation. But for a tiny minority, selectively destined for university English, the S-level papers, with their indeterminate syllabus and their provocations to critical adventurousness, afford a glimpse of the larger liberties of the academy.

For what else is that long process of educational assessment and competitive selection but a means of discriminating those who will in their turn enjoy the right to discriminate on their own account? Consider the social composition of GCE streams, of sixth forms, of university departments, and the separated meanings run irresistibly together. Beneath the disinterested procedures of literary judgement and discrimination can be discerned the outlines of other, harsher words: exclusion, subordination, dispossession.

### Uses of literacy

> The [middle-class] child has a choice of determining his own action. He can, if *he* prefers, play with his toys. The working-class order tends in the opposite direction. 'You do what I tell you.' The real point is this: the world to the middle-class child does make sense and he can learn about it through language. . . . He is open to imaginative and rational communication – a real type of education can begin.
>
> (Abbs 1969, p. 32)

Behind *these* astonishingly crude discriminations lie not only the complacent prejudice and ignorance of the bourgeois educator but also, more importantly, the influential sociolinguistics of Basil Bernstein; and the passage shows clearly the way in which Bernstein's speculations about 'restricted' and 'elaborated' codes (see Bernstein 1971) – which in 1967 Quintin Hoare called 'genuinely revolutionary' in their impact (Hoyles 1977,

p. 49) – may assume in the context of a Leavisite hatred of 'mass civilization' an entirely different character. For Leavis's hostility to all aspects of the mass media and the consumer society can, like Arnold's and James's in their time, slide all too easily into a fastidious and uncomprehending distaste for working-class life, represented, often, in shockingly oversimplified fashion.

Peter Abbs, who has written widely on the creative uses of English teaching, represents one tendency within 'progressivism'. Of course, progressive English teaching is a broad church, embracing many different and contradictory positions and practices. For every Abbs, infatuated with the cognitive superiority of middle-class English, there is a Leila Berg or Chris Searle mobilizing the linguistic and cultural resources of working-class children. All would place a high value on literature, as on literacy. But their understandings of those words, and of their practical utilities, would diverge very widely indeed. An understanding of these divergences, even within such a relatively homogeneous activity as English teaching, requires some consideration of the history of English in schools over the past fifty years.

This chapter has argued that in its formative period, from 1860 to 1930, the teaching of reading and writing finds its ultimate sanction in a pedagogically determined articulation of the standard language and the national literature. But the subsequent history suggests that the relations between the two practices have been a good deal more complicated than that. Even Newbolt, while asserting the hypothetical unity of literacy and literature, was obliged to concede regretfully that the latter 'no longer springs from the life of the people' and 'is not generally recognized as having any direct bearing on their life' (Newbolt 1921, p. 256). When the Newbolt exhortations found a cooler and more practical embodiment in the Hadow Report of 1926, that central unity was dismantled and recomposed in terms of an education system moving firmly towards curricular specialization and the formal institution of different types and levels of schooling. The hegemony of standard English remains, of course, and the education reports of the thirties continue to gesture with pious vagueness towards the 'civilizing effects' of a literary education. But the effective stress has shifted decisively elsewhere. Education is seen to serve not an Arnoldian conception of 'culture' (though R. H. Tawney, for example, continued, like his friend Lindsay, to argue for something of the kind), but a newer conception of practical 'citizenship'. Literature finds itself rudely jostled in the school curriculum by upstart subjects better tuned to the modernity and pragmatism of that concept: history, geography, domestic science, current affairs, civics:

> A man may be splendidly educated as a technician, capable of doing valuable work in his vocation; he may be a profound scholar, an authority on some literary and artistic subject, and yet may be uneducated as a member of his community, knowing nothing and caring nothing about the lives of his fellow citizens, incapable of fulfilling his function as a responsible citizen in a democratic state.
>
> (Simon 1936, Preface)

In 1935 the *Education Yearbook* seconded Newbolt's misgivings about the general relevance of literary culture and liberal education, but this time with relish rather than regret:

> A four-hundred-year tradition of literary culture and education has failed to produce a literary people, even in the country which prides itself upon possessing the finest literature in the world. . . . The attraction of wireless and the film lies in the sense that their audiences have that they are in contact with something real and spontaneous rather than something second-hand and academic.

Shame of shames! Literature 'second-hand and academic'? Against this, *Scrutiny* continued to insist on the primacy of literature as a focus of 'moral and cultural problems', as 'the point from which all education must take its start' (L. C. Knights, in *Scrutiny*, 2, 2 (1933), p. 153). But even there the pejorative force of 'academic' can increasingly be felt. Faced with evidence like the above of cultural 'betrayal', *Scrutiny*'s intense early preoccupation with schools and the training of teachers had given way, by the middle of the decade, to a despairing withdrawal into what Leavis was already calling, as early as 1934, 'the idea of the university' (*Scrutiny*, 3, 1 (1934), p. 130).

*Scrutiny*'s defensive retrenchment in the mid-thirties forms part of a general 'migration' of literary ideology into higher education. Not, of course, a mechanical segregation between school and university, but a marked divergence none the less: literacy for citizenship in the schools, literature for the specialized few in the universities – the latter producing in this period a notable efflorescence of literary-critical activity, to be canonized later as the 'New Criticism'. But if the Hadow and Spens reports helped articulate some of the dominant assumptions of the 1944 Act – the validity of psychometric testing, the institutional differentiation of secondary schooling, the importance of practical and technical pedagogies – the schools presided over by that Act counted among their staff substantial numbers of young 'Leavisites', heirs to *Scrutiny*'s passionate ethical preoccupation with the survival of literary traditions. And if they inherited the journal's evangelism they inherited too, often enough, its élitism, its cultural despair, its intolerant hatred of 'mass civilization'. The New Criticism forged in the academies of England and North America became the 'practical criticism' of the secondary schools of the 1950s. What had started out as a radical provocation to the 'old gang', the *belles-lettristes* of Oxbridge and the Royal Society of Literature, was becoming, a generation later, a new establishment.

The literary-cultural struggles of the thirties bequeathed to the post-war years a tissue of paradoxical outcomes. The socialist Orwell allowed his name to be subscribed without protest to cold-war posturings of the most reactionary kind. Leavisite poachers turned gamekeepers *en masse*, a move facilitated by the cultural chauvinism and anti-communism of the master. As for the broader shift, already noted in the thirties – a shift that displaces literature from its curricular pre-eminence and redefines literacy in terms of other measures of social value and utility – that too can be followed through to the fifties and sixties, though not without some significant alteration of the key words. The mild jacobinism of 'citizenship' gives ground, in the heyday of British social democracy, to the more elusive and vaguely reassuring notion of 'community'.

> The field in which it is most important that ordinary boys and girls should learn to exercise a common sense judgement quickened by imaginative insight is that of personal relations. Their greatest service to the community, and there is none

> greater, will be as men and women who can be relied on to make a success of their own lives and by the quality of their living to bring up their children to do the same.
> (Central Advisory Council for Education 1963, p. 113)

And what are the school subjects that will help ensure this laudable outcome?

> Here, then, is a vital core of interest ready to hand. And educators need have no hesitation in using it as the central theme and motive for new curricula. . . . For there is a wide agreement that a man's understanding of himself, and of Man, is of the first importance in the education of ordinary pupils. . . . How can all be brought up to have some kind of hold on their personal lives, and on their place in, and contribution to, the various communities – family, neighbourhood, club, occupational, national and international, in which they play a part?
> (Schools Council 1965, p. 10)

The 'apostles of culture', battling on grimly but undaunted in a cultural wasteland of current affairs, communications studies and ROSLA projects, may perhaps have permitted themselves an ironic satisfaction at this deft appropriation of their vocabulary. For, if the liberal educationists of the sixties were still concerned with what I. A. Richards had called 'the expansion and dissolution of our communities' (Richards 1964, p. 350), they most certainly did not share his conviction that the remedy lay in 'the critical reading of poetry'.

> The view of the curriculum put forward in this paper is therefore holistic. It is suggested that it should possess organic unity, and that the organizing principle most likely to provide a sound basis for development is the study of Man, and of human society, needs and purposes.
> (Schools Council 1965, p. 12)

While Richards might have applauded their determination to 'find means of exercising our power of choice', it is less certain that he would have approved their sense of the relevant texts:

> The ability to discriminate between pop music which is mawkish, sentimental or boring, and that which evokes,

> however crudely, genuine human feeling, represents a gain in sensitivity that is worth having. . . . The ability to see, however dimly, that the pay packet is not the only possible criterion for industrial action.
>
> (Schools Council 1965, p. 12)

Easy to scoff at this, no doubt. But this version of 'discrimination', whose rather naïvely instrumental relation to social-democratic containment is plain to see, has none the less a more progressive social content than the infinitely more sophisticated literary discriminations discussed earlier. The Schools Council, established in 1964 to supervise curriculum development and to relate it to educational research and to 'the general interest of the community, both local and national, in the educational process', was seen by some teachers as a threat to their professional autonomy. But in practice, in a period of educational expansion, of Plowden-inspired 'educational priority areas' and of the institution of the Certificate of Secondary Education, and given its corporate hostility to the traditional subject curriculum and its encouragement of cross-disciplinary topic work, the Schools Council helped to loosen the stranglehold of the university examining and matriculation boards and to create in some state schools a space for innovation and experiment which had hitherto been confined almost entirely to private ventures like Bedales, Summerhill and Beacon Hill.

'Progressive teaching', as we have said, is a hopelessly baggy term, covering a range of very different things from a neo-Leavisite conception of creativity and self-discovery through literature (Peter Abbs, David Holbrook), often accompanied by a marked distaste for the actual lived culture of most children, to actively socialist and feminist and libertarian interventions in curriculum and teaching style. Perhaps the latter would now disown the label 'progressive'. Certainly it has often concealed a very ambiguous relation to the language and experience of working-class children. In one version, those children are seen as culturally and linguistically 'deprived' or 'disadvantaged', and the job of the school is to 'compensate' for that deprivation. In another, superficially more 'radical', variant, the child's culture is granted, in theory, equal validity with the dominant culture of the school, and the teacher's task is to develop an anthropological neutrality or 'multiculturalism'. In practice, the results of the two attitudes have tended, as Martin Hoyles observes, to be similar:

> The aim is still the same: to enter mainstream culture, which, if it means high culture, is ironically a minority culture. Simply, the process has become more subtle. Each child is seen as having his own culture which must be respected, but it is not suggested that middle-class children be initiated into working-class culture, or whites into black culture.
>
> (Hoyles 1977, p. 178)

The dishonesty of this is evidently not lost on the children themselves, numbers of whom rather persistently decline (or 'fail') to respond to the noble aspirations of their teachers. The fledgling Schools Council soon ran into disconcerting evidence of 'conflict and misunderstanding' between what it called 'the short-term viewpoints of parents and pupils who are concerned with starting work in the immediate future' and 'the long-term objectives of teachers who see their responsibility as preparing pupils for the whole of their future lives (Schools Council 1968, p. 45). Indeed, this regrettable indifference to what the Council called 'ethical values' was even expressed as a preference for such 'practical aspects of everyday living' as 'being able to speak well and easily and to put things in writing easily' (Schools Council 1968, p. 35) – a definition of literacy (or 'eloquence') that the humanist educators of the Renaissance would not have been ashamed to offer to their aristocratic patrons. The whirligig of time brings in its revenges!

## The politics of reading and writing

Teachers are caught, here, in a tissue of intractable contradictions. Indeed, it is one of the illusions of the epoch that the educational system can bring into harmony, singlehanded, the antagonistic social forces of capitalist society – an illusion that socialist teachers, whether as socialists or as teachers, can ill afford to share. And it is the contradictions that need, at this stage, to be stressed. 'Systematic training in the use of standard English' has proved one of the most effective ways in which the exploited classes, child and adult, have been induced to consent to the conditions of their own cultural subordination. Common observation will confirm how often the upwardly mobile working-class child, the 'scholarship boy' (or girl), has proved a durable recruit to the ideologies and the rewards of capital, and how the attendant sacrifice and loss of connection have seemed, to those left behind, matter for pride and celebration as much as regret. But literacy is a weapon too, a form of cultural power, gained in struggle and, in the 1860s and 1870s, conceded as much as given.

Similarly, too, literature, with its faithful amanuensis 'criticism', undoubtedly embodies and transmits the social-aesthetic values of white male bourgeois society, values whose protestations of purity and disinterestedness have scarcely bothered to conceal the ugliness and exploitation that lie close at hand. But literature in the broader sense of poem, story, play is also a powerful source of knowledge, of history, and hence of challenge and resistance. Palgrave and Tennyson revered 'the noble language of Shelley'. But so did the proletarian communists of the 1830s, for different reasons. Literary critics have allowed themselves at last, after a century of fastidious disapproval, to value the novels of Dickens. Many working-class readers did so from the start, finding in them, it may be, an answering anger and a powerful laughter. 'Learn your letters,' declared Bertolt Brecht. 'They're not enough, but still learn them.' Or again: 'Grab hold of the book, you hungry one. It's a weapon' ('In Praise of Learning', in *The Mother*, Brecht 1978).

It is important to recognize and honour such alternative traditions of popular literacy. But it is equally important, if that recognition is to be more than merely rhetorical, to admit that they have little to do with schooling, nurtured as they were within the political and familial cultures of the nineteenth-century working class, and that the school curriculum has to a very large extent displaced and usurped them. Education remains, in the age of radio, film and television, far and away the most powerful of the cultural apparatuses. If the curriculum, in Bernstein's words, 'defines what counts as valid knowledge' (Bernstein 1977), then the linguistic practices of standard English that preside over it from first to last and that permeate its pedagogies and its rituals of evaluation are validated and revalidated continuously, how many millions of times a day:

continuously *and* absolutely, since, as the practical medium of the pedagogic process, standard English appears not as a particular historical practice of language with its own appropriate occasions and limits of usefulness, but as *the* language itself, the neutral and unchanging norm (for what else does 'standard' mean?) by which all other practices are judged, as quaint or deplorable, as idiom or jargon, as dialect or abuse.

In France that norm has been regulated with Thermidorian efficiency by the lexical gendarmerie of the Académie Française. In Britain, when the schools fail, as in the heyday of progressivism they were held to be deliberately and culpably failing on a large scale, we rely typically on a self-appointed citizen constabulary of linguistic pundits and amateur lexicologists. But above all the authority of standard English still derives from its historical if unevenly articulated alliance with the national literature, or rather 'Literature', since that too becomes, in the same process, a curricular selection and organization of 'valid knowledge', with the implicit devalidation of everything that lies outside its field.

The size and shape of that field has varied a good deal, depending on where you stand and when. Under the regime of *Scrutiny* it threatened to contract to the scale and the weedless formal regularity of a suburban front garden. During the sixties it expanded, in higher education at least, into a genial colonialism, with a relaxation of Leavisite immigration controls (American studies, Commonwealth literature) and the development of outlying dependencies (women's studies, cultural studies, sociologies of literature), some of which have subsequently 'gone native' in rather alarming ways. But whatever its scope, and regardless of its precise position at any moment within the overall curricular economy, the primary function of literature is still, as it was for Arnold and Newbolt and Eliot, to 'purify the dialect of the tribe': to provide an absolute discursive authority for the educational and social prestige of standard English.

Left-wing teachers frequently resent arguments of this kind. It is understandable that, from within the immediate and often extremely rewarding experience of reading *Kes* or *Zigger Zagger* or *The Loneliness of the Long Distance Runner* with a group of lively 14-year-olds, the lofty claim that schooling, whatever the teacher's views and intentions, always and inevitably reproduces the hegemony of standard English and the dominant cultural order simply confirms their sense of the insulting remoteness and mandarin irrelevance of academic 'theory'. But such a sense, though no doubt justified in particular cases, is also dangerously limited and, above all, vulnerable. Certainly it can no longer be plausible, after the débâcles of Risinghill and William Tyndale[7] and now the savage financial and ideological assaults on comprehensive schooling, to sustain the illusion of the classroom and the curriculum as a 'secret garden', a domain of freedom. If those teachers would reject such a notion in favour of a more active conception of oppositional schooling, they might none the less consider as a matter not of theory but of ordinary observation and reflection whether the structures and processes of social power do not only encompass but actively penetrate and permeate the school at every level: in the social relations of staffroom and classroom, in the 'invisible pedagogies' of the curriculum, in the routines of organization and assessment that point beyond the horizon of the school towards the stubborn materialities of the social and sexual division of labour.

'Invisible pedagogies' is Bernstein's phrase (Bernstein 1975); and in this respect it is possible that his work, first welcomed and then harshly repudiated by progressives, and even denounced for helping to reinforce the linguistic subordination of working-class children, may now be coming to be seen only to enjoin a necessary realism. Even that notorious distinction between restricted and elaborated codes, despite the valuable work that it prompted, by way of refutation, on the expressiveness and structural complexity of non-standard language, can be understood as an attempt to grasp the relations of linguistic power *within* the school, relations embedded in the deep structures of the curriculum and the school system. For it should by now be evident that educational standard English, far from being a homogeneous 'common' language, articulates different and contradictory linguistic practices – simple and complex sentences, elementary and secondary literacy – which serve to underpin and naturalize differentials of performance, achievement and destination within a notionally comprehensive institution. For all the impressive work done under the auspices of the CSE, in particular in its non-examination mode three,

English language at GCE Ordinary level (interesting name: what proportion of the 'ordinary' school population ever takes, let alone passes it?) remains the turnstile that regulates access to higher education and thence to the 'choice' between job (or joblessness) and career, between manual and mental occupations. Standing as it does at the intersection of two modes of literacy, it represents a concrete manifestation of the contradictions and ambiguities of social-democratic education: schooling for 'equality' and schooling for the 'needs of the economy'. And those contradictions point in their turn to still more fundamental antagonisms, whose causes, and whose eventual resolutions, may remind us that questions of literature and language, for all their urgent and necessary specificity, must take their place within an altogether wider struggle.

# 3
# Fiction as politics: working-class writing in the inter-war years

The struggles to establish the hegemony of liberal-humanist definitions of literature within education, outlined above, have not been restricted to the areas of state schooling and higher education. From the turn of the century until the Second World War, and once again more recently, the nature and function of literature have been contested in working-class education and left-wing cultural politics. This contest has taken the form of challenging the restricted access to culture in its liberal-humanist definition in our society and of producing alternative radical definitions of culture in which literature has a political role to play in the mobilization of opposition to exploitation. In this context, developments in working-class writing have been central.

This chapter is concerned with this alternative strand of cultural history. It attempts to understand the cultural-political context of working-class writing in the inter-war years by examining the ways in which that writing was conceived in educational and left-wing cultural debate. Yet the questions with which it is concerned are of more than historical interest. They remain central to the recent renaissance of working-class writing and developments in black and feminist writing in the alternative and community publishing sectors. Those involved in these forms of cultural-political activity find themselves faced, in a different context, with questions about reading and writing, politics and ideology, similar to those confronted by working-class writing in the twenties and thirties. They include questions of form and content, and of the relationship between reading, writing and political struggle. Those involved must face, too, the problem of marginalization, and the relationship of 'alternative' and 'oppositional' writing to the dominant cultural order in both its highbrow and popular forms. It is with an understanding of these issues in the inter-war period and today that this chapter is concerned.

*

> He [Arthur Horner, President of the South Wales Miners' Federation] suggested that the full meaning of life in the Welsh mining areas could be expressed for the general reader more truthfully and vividly, if treated imaginatively, than by any amount of statistical and historical research. What I have set out to do, therefore, is to 'novelise' (if I may use the term) a phase of working-class history. All events described, though not placed in chronological order, have occurred, each of them marks a milestone in the lives and struggles of the South Wales Miners.
>
> (Jones 1937, Foreword)

From the end of the nineteenth century until the Second World War, the term 'working-class writing' was used to describe a variety of texts written by amateur or initially amateur writers from an industrial working-class background.[8] The term 'proletarian writing' was also widely used in the same way, though on the Marxist left it signified writing which was explicitly class-conscious. As descriptive categories, the two terms can be found variously in press reviews, publishers' catalogues, labour and adult education journals and radical literary magazines. Interest in working-class writing was largely confined to sections of the labour movement and the intelligentsia. It remained marginal to the literary traditions defined by professional critics in the universities, and had no place in the dominant literary discourse, which insisted on the absolute separation of literature, politics and ideology.

During the inter-war period the number and range of texts published varied, as did their reception, according to changes in the broader social relationships which created the conditions for the production and consumption of writing. Developments in education were of key importance, in particular the formation through adult education of new and varied reading publics and the development of the debate on literature, politics and socialism which adult education organizations helped to promote. Important, too, were the expansion of libraries, the development of a particular kind of left-wing intelligentsia under the auspices of the Popular Front, and the increased interest among commercial publishers in working-class writing.

The term 'working-class writing' tells us very little about the style, subject-matter or perspective of the literature it is used to describe. Whatever the expectations of socialists in the period, there was no 'natural' working-class ideological perspective. Just like the writing of other classes and social groups, working-class writing in the twenties and thirties was shaped by both dominant and oppositional ideological practices, which it variously affirmed and contested. In addition to class, it was subject to a range of other determinations including gender and regional and political difference. While the texts in question often represented aspects of working-class social and political organization, they also reproduced elements from those dominant discourses which masked differences of class and gender and promoted a seemingly shared system of beliefs and values that was supposedly the heritage of all citizens.

In its formal features, working-class writing was subject to the influence of already existing ideas about good writing and literary style, ideas transmitted through school, adult education and general reading, and encompassing both popular and 'literary' forms. These ideas in turn were shaped by the assumptions of publishers, the response of critics and the influence of sympathetic literary intellectuals, all of whose views had been moulded by powerful educational and cultural values.

Between 1918 and 1938, a considerable number of novels, autobiographies, documentary pieces and short stories by working-class writers were published by mainstream publishers as well as in liberal and left-wing educational and cultural journals. Their authors came from a broad range of industrial workers and from the unemployed. There was a particular concentration of writers in the mining communities, a phenomenon best understood in terms of the particular social organization and educational traditions of the colliery districts. Formal education had often been limited, for working-class writers, to the completion of minimum elementary schooling, but many were involved in some way in adult education. The life of an industrial worker is not conducive, in practical terms, to writing, and these authors found it difficult to interest a commercial publisher. Commercially published working-class writing was almost exclusively the work of men. Not only were women usually burdened with the dual role of wage-earner and housewife-mother, but strongly-held attitudes to women's role effectively prevented their active participation in political and intellectual life. There was better representation of the writing of working-class women in journals – which suggests that material constraints made it easier for them to write short pieces.

Most working-class writing between the wars has a marked regional character, drawing on the history and social conditions of the areas in which it is set. Class-based inequality is an explicit theme of this writing, while patriarchal relations are more often portrayed as natural. Racial oppression, where present as a theme, is given by the specific context of the writing. Thus, for example, Ken Worpole has recently drawn attention to an important tradition of Jewish fiction which explicitly raised questions of race, often in the context of the anti-fascist struggle in Spain and the threat of Mosley's blackshirts at home (Worpole 1983).

Articles and reviews about working-class writing of the period are dominated by the literary ideology of realism. Texts must be 'true to life'. The prestige of realism was further underlined for many working-class writers by its privileged status in left-wing aesthetics and cultural politics, and by the influence of new concepts of 'socialist realism' in the Soviet Union after the 1934 Writers' Congress.[9] The commonest formal device in working-class fiction is thus the omniscient narrator, who sees everything and shares it with the reader, silently imposing a point of view and a set of values. In some texts the narrator intervenes with evaluative comment, or the protagonist assumes a particular political perspective. But generally politics as a theme is not central, and the characters are shown to live out the effects of political and economic forces – strikes, unemployment, inequality – at the level of personal life rather than of collective organization.

It was assumed that the realistic representation of the poverty and suffering of working people, and their experience and achievement in industrial and political struggle, constituted in itself a political statement. As a subject for fiction, this material went rather beyond the boundaries of literary decorum and good taste, without having the direct and less decorous appeal of popular thrillers and romances. Nevertheless, a good deal of working-class poetry and fiction found its way into print in the period, and most publishers had a token working-class writer on their lists. By the mid-thirties publishers were actually advertising for working-class authors, and their books were marketed both as 'human interest' stories and as shocking revelations of the conditions of working-class life. Only left-wing publishers like Gollancz promoted them for their political interest and value. Working-class fiction was reviewed in mainstream literary journals like *The Times Literary Supplement*, in adult education papers like *The Plebs* and *The Highway*, and in journals of the left like the *New Statesman*, the *Left Review* and the *Sunday Worker*. Radical adult education throughout the period, and from 1934 onwards the Writers' International, helped to create a readership for working-class writing.

This chapter focuses on the cultural and political context of working-class writing as it was defined in debates about literature, cultural politics and socialism in three journals: *The Plebs*, published by the Plebs League; *The Highway*, the paper of the Workers' Educational Association; and the *Left Review*, the organ of the British section of the Writers' International.[10] We also look briefly at *Literature of World Revolution*, published by the Soviet-based International Bureau of Proletarian and Revolutionary Writers, and at *New Writing*, a literary periodical produced by John Lehmann. Apart from fiction and poetry themselves, most of these publications also gave space to discussions of literature and politics, discussions which helped to create a general political climate for the reception of working-class writing and the debates about it.

The degree of interest shown on the left in the politics of culture fluctuated in the years from 1918 to 1938. During the twenties, literature and art were of only minor interest on the left. The Marxist intelligentsia operated with an economistic form of Marxist theory which downgraded the importance of culture and ideology and concentrated on economic modes of analysis and political activity, while in the mainstream of the labour movement literature was seen as a means to the moral and spiritual development of the individual, and thus as a precondition for social change. In the trade unions and the Labour Party the immediate cultural-political priority was education. The indifference of most bourgeois literary intellectuals to left-wing cultural and political issues meant that there was no strong pressure group actively urging the consideration of questions of literature and politics from a left perspective. Yet even in the twenties some debate of those issues did take place, in the adult education journals and in particular in the most radical of them, *The Plebs*. This debate was at its most animated in the earlier part of the decade, under the influence of developments at home and in the Soviet Union. In these years *The Plebs* raised fundamental questions about literature, class and politics for a largely working-class readership.

It was not until 1934 that a significant number of middle-class intellectuals with time and money at their disposal became interested in the politics of literature and culture. The sectarian political climate on the left in the years before the Popular Front – a climate which was at its strongest between 1929 and 1933 – had been disastrous for the formation of a radical intelligentsia in Britain.[11] The British Communist Party was small, and its members were prevented by the policy of the Comintern from making alliances with other parties and organizations on the left, many of which that policy denounced as 'social fascist'. It was not until 1933–4, with the shift in Moscow to a 'frontist' strategy against (real) fascism, that a broadly based branch of the Writers' International could be formed in Britain, embracing both working-class and middle-class writers and literary intellectuals. Its journal, the *Left Review*, became the main forum of debate within this movement until 1938.

During the twenties, any success that working-class writers had achieved had been in spite of the attitude of the labour movement, and sometimes in the face of very negative criticism in the labour press. The new left intelligentsia of the later thirties set out to encourage working-class participation in the arts, and were able to open up some new outlets for working-class writing. The *Left Review, International Literature* and *New Writing* all published short pieces of prose and poetry by working-class writers, and publishers began to show more interest in their work. This in turn was part of new interest in working-class life, attested also by the documentary film movement, by Madge and Harrison's 'Mass Observation' and by the journalism of Orwell.[12]

## Education, literature and working-class writing

From the turn of the century until the Second World War the provision of elementary state education remained basic and regionally uneven, in spite of the recommendations of a series of Education Acts, the most part of which remained unimplemented. This, and the severely limited access of the majority of the population to any kind of education after 14, helped create a substantial demand for adult education which was met both by self-education and by a number of organizations with widely differing political and educational aims. These included university extension classes, local-authority adult education classes, courses run by the Co-operative Movement, the WEA, by political parties, trade unions, private schools and by the Plebs League and the National Council of Labour Colleges. Many of these organizations offered both direct teaching and correspondence courses. Demand for adult education was further strengthened by the high value placed on education in the labour movement. Many of its participant organizations saw education, more widely and equally distributed, as the key to social justice and political change. On the whole, however, with the exception of the Marxist left, socialists and labour movement intellectuals did not question what was meant by 'education'. They simply took over the dominant definition of education, as a process of individual self-development, transcending limitations of class position and unconcerned with differences of political viewpoint.

The 'individual' assumed in this definition is thus classless, but not ungendered, since the same conception of education often ascribes a different 'natural' disposition and potential to women and men. On the left of the labour movement, however, in the Labour Colleges and the educational activities of the Independent Labour Party and the Communist Party, education was differently defined, as predominantly a political issue, a weapon in the class struggle. Here the dominant assumptions about the meaning and value of education were put in question. What sort of education should be provided, and for whom? Here too theoretical understandings began to be developed of the relations between existing educational institutions and syllabuses and the dominant ideological and political structures.

These divergent definitions of the nature and purpose of education led to fundamental differences in the content and method of adult education classes. We are concerned here with the effects of these differences on the teaching of literature and literacy, and with the ways in which the work of producing a reading and writing public, begun in elementary schooling, was completed or redefined in adult education. The teaching of literature and literacy brought with it attitudes, both implicit and explicit, to the politics of culture, and in particular to reading and writing as political activities. By looking in some detail at *The Highway* and *The Plebs*, we focus on the WEA and the Labour College movement, the two largest and most influential adult education organizations with direct relations to the trade unions and the wider labour movement. These two organizations held sharply opposed positions on education, and competed for students and trade-union affiliations. Both published a regular paper, in which, among other things, they promoted their views on the place of literature in education and national life. Both, too, published, reviewed and commented on working-class writing. We should remember, however, that, although the official position of the two organizations is represented in *The Highway* and *The Plebs*, actual practice locally, in the WEA especially, did not always conform very closely to that position.

## The WEA and *The Highway*

> The WEA and the Labour Movement have a common outlook on education. We have rivalled each other in our attack on that commercialising, enslaving, soul-destroying

> conception which has too long passed for education. We have joined forces in our demand for the establishment of a system which would nurture and give freedom to all those powers which go to the making of men and women and 'citizens of rare quality'.
>
> (*The Highway*, 14, 5 (1922), p. 75)

> It is believed by many that this appetite for knowledge is actuated by the search for a political end – that is, that those workers seeking knowledge value it only as a weapon in their 'struggle for emancipation'. However much truth there may be in this applied to occasional individuals, for most people it is truer to say that the possession of knowledge and an active intellect are themselves the evidence of, rather than the means to, emancipation in the true sense.
>
> (*The Highway*, 16, 3 (1924), p. 118)

> The WEA, in its origins a 'humanitarian effort', accepts the viewpoint that 'education is above the battle'. Its often-pleaded defence – that as a matter of actual fact its tutors are at liberty to see to it 'that the type of education given is more revolutionary than would meet with the approval of the Board of Education or universities' – is shown to involve the throwing overboard of the 'non-political and non-partisan' character of the organization and the giving up of the pretence that education takes no sides.
>
> (*The Plebs*, 13, 1 (1921), p. 2)

The Workers' Educational Association was founded in 1903 with the aim of providing an education for adult working-class students which would unite the principles of a liberal education of the kind informing much university extension teaching with the moral precepts of co-operation.[13] The association expanded rapidly, and by the end of the First World War had 209 branches and 14,697 individual members. It attracted support from non-Marxist socialists, trade-unionists, professional educationalists, churchmen and members of parliament, all of whom were represented on the WEA council. The association was founded on the principle of the political neutrality of education, a principle strictly adhered to and constantly reaffirmed in the editorials in *The Highway* and the annual address to the council.

It was the basis of the WEA's respectability, and the precondition for financial support from government. This support was dependent on the vetting of courses by government inspectors. At the local level, however, the effectiveness of this kind of central supervision is doubtful, since the responsibility for teaching methods and materials lay with individual tutors, many of whom were radical in opinions and method. The WEA laid much stress on education for citizenship, but insisted on different roles and educational needs for men and women, in a society in which women were not fully enfranchised until 1928. Women students, while not actually excluded from other classes, were offered special courses in domestic skills, intended to serve as a preparation for marriage and motherhood.

The WEA took an active interest in education at all levels. It was energetic in helping to shape and support the liberal recommendation of the 1918 Education Act, and critical of the failure to implement the wide-ranging recommendations of this and later Acts. It opposed cuts in the universities, and campaigned for better cultural facilities and libraries for working people. In all these respects its efforts were directed towards the *extension* of existing provision rather than fundamental change in the structure, content and definition of education; and both in its policies and its organizational hierarchies the WEA was – and has remained – an organization *for* rather than *of* the working class, in which middle-class professionals defined the character and limits of legitimate working-class interests and needs. So constituted, with its carefully deferential relation to education and 'culture', the WEA served to contain and defuse stronger and more radical demands from the left of the labour movement, helping to meet claims for equality of opportunity, and providing politicians and educationists with a means of raising 'better citizens'.

This insistence on the political neutrality of education, and the accompanying belief in the improving social effects of a liberal education, created an educational attitude conducive to the incorporation of the dominant literary discourse of the period and congenial to the central role of literature courses in the WEA curriculum. Throughout the inter-war years the WEA placed great emphasis on the role of literature in education, and promoted the dominant literary and cultural values to its working-class students. Literature was offered to them as the repository of universal truths and values, of all that was best in human culture, and as providing the intellectual and moral training necessary to the citizens of a democracy. The perspective that informs most commentary on literature in *The Highway* is conservative: the study of literature is the study of life, promoting 'true understanding' and bringing 'real culture' to the deprived and so creating standards of cultural consumption and response to counteract the depredations of 'mass culture'.

The WEA's high estimation of the role of literature can be seen as an extension of assumptions about the cultural significance of the literary tradition which have pervaded British intellectual life since Arnold, assumptions which we discussed in Chapter 2, and which ascribe to literature the power to create a national unity on the basis of shared values and a common language. Thus WEA literature classes studied texts of the established literary tradition, extending it to include modern writers like Shaw and Galsworthy. The importance ascribed to literature can be seen clearly in articles and reviews in *The Highway*, where fiction and literary criticism featured strongly. There is a strong contrast here with *The Plebs*, whose aim was to develop a Marxist understanding of literature. In *The Highway*, however varied the tone and viewpoint of the reviews, the central conceptions of literature remain orthodox.

This attitude to literature had implications for working-class writing. If literature is concerned with the truth about life and the preservation of universal insights and values, the class background of the writer is clearly unimportant. The major aim of the association was to ensure that working-class women and men *read* literature, not that they should write it. There were socialists in the WEA who argued for the function of literature as an agent of social and moral enlightenment: if novels and poems could portray the 'truth' of working-class life, then literature could also compel its readers to acknowledge the need for change. This strand in WEA thinking, though subordinated to the Arnoldian conception of literary culture, was responsible for occasional articles about working-class fiction and for a few favourable reviews of it – though not, needless to say, of the more committed examples.

## The NCLC and *The Plebs*

> The 'impartial education' idea has its source in a very 'partial' quarter, and so long as the control of education comes from that quarter, the working-class movement will be poisoned and drained.
>
> (*The Plebs' Magazine*, 1, 4 (1909), p. 63)

> University life is the breeding-ground of reaction. It incites by its very nature towards breaking away from working-class aspirations and cleaving unto the class above. The knowledge that is to be of any service to the Labour Movement is not to be gained in that quarter.
>
> (*The Plebs' Magazine*, 1, 3 (1909), p. 44)

The WEA's main rivals in the field of adult education were the Plebs League and the National Council of Labour Colleges. The Plebs League was founded in 1908 after a dispute at Ruskin College over the content of the syllabus, which the students considered too conservative.[14] The dispute led to the establishment of an autonomous adult education movement. Its aims were to promote independent socialist working-class education, to found a Labour College and to produce a journal, first called *The Plebs' Magazine* and from 1919 onwards *The Plebs*. The motto of the movement was 'Educate to Organize', indicating its unashamedly political and partisan intentions. Branches were founded all over the country, owned and controlled by working people and offering an alternative to the 'impartiality' provided by the WEA and university extension lectures.

Through *The Plebs*, which carried articles on a wide range of political, educational, scientific and cultural issues, the movement set out to establish a new understanding of the structure, content and aims of education. It challenged the WEA's policy of extending existing kinds of education to working people, questioning their relevance to the labour movement and the class struggle. The scholarship system came in for particularly fierce attack, as a means of kidnapping working-class intellectuals and turning them against their class. The Plebs League, and the associated National Council of Labour Colleges, were self-financing, relying mainly on levies from affiliated trade unions. The annual council and the magazine were the main forum for formulation of policy. The movement offered taught and correspondence courses, along with day, weekend and summer schools. It trained its own tutors and published its own textbooks and pamphlets on political issues. In its refusal to accept the distinction between education and politics, the Labour College movement is the closest thing we had in this period to the training of cadres, of a stratum of Gramscian 'organic intellectuals' dedicated to the establishment of a 'proletarian order'. Certainly it embodied the strongest challenge to the educational consensus until the Second World War.

From the outset the Plebs League stressed the importance of educating women in the same way as men. This unusual denial of sexual difference can be understood in part as a defensive response to the growing importance in those years of feminist agitation and the women's movement. It represents an attempt to prevent working-class women from identifying their interests outside the labour movement, as well as a reflection of Marxist thinking on 'the woman question'.[15] *The Plebs* stressed that sexual inequality was the product of economic inequality, a result of the capitalist system under which working-class women were the oppressed of the oppressed. Equality rather than difference between the sexes was the emphasis; and, while this meant that women and men should be treated equally in the labour movement, it veiled those structural relations of power and powerlessness that frame relationships between the sexes, which cannot be fully accounted for merely in economic terms. It was these forms of patriarchal relations, which are not specific to capitalist societies and which will not automatically disappear with them, that were rendered invisible. This failure to appreciate the specificity of gender, characteristic of the left in the period, had important consequences for women's participation in educational and political activity. No attempt was made to challenge the sexual division of labour and the double exploitation of women, with the result that they had to struggle themselves to redefine their role and claim their right to play a full part in the movement. As one woman protested in *The Plebs*:

> I've washed up for peace, I've washed up for socialism, I've washed up for disarmament, but I'm not going to wash up for education, because I want to be in the class and not at the sink.
>
> (*The Plebs*, 20, 1 (1928), p. 13)

The explicitly political stance taken by the Labour College movement led to a fundamental questioning of what should be taught to working-class students, and of who should teach it. As a matter of principle, courses were aimed at helping students understand the society and the world in which they lived, so as to be able to change it. An attempt was made to develop a Marxist approach to the various disciplines, through a revaluation of the form and content of teaching and the production of new textbooks. The emphasis on political usefulness meant that the main subjects were economics, history and geography, together with practically oriented courses on local government, trade unions, election work and labour organization.

In this context, literature did not figure prominently. Until the end of the First World War it played a very minor part in the league. Educationally it was seen to be firmly located within the bourgeois ideology of liberal education to which the league was resolutely opposed. In the magazine, however, it began to figure more and more prominently as a worthwhile leisure pursuit. The absence of literature from the serious education programme, and its relocation in the private domain of leisure and personal culture, has, of course, always been a feature of the labour movement, and was not in any way challenged by the economistic Marxism of the period. Thus, in spite of its hostility to both the WEA and the Newbolt ideology of liberal education, the Plebs League did virtually nothing to challenge the conventional assessment of the nature and value of literature. Tutors and students aware of the bourgeois character and reactionary pretensions of the literary canon could only move into an outright rejection of all literature as unredeemably bourgeois and reactionary. In this way, an important area of struggle was conceded by default.

In the twenties, however, *The Plebs* began to develop an analysis of literature which, while sharply critical of its ideological purposes and uses, did not concede it entirely to the class enemy. It acknowledged the need for a Marxist understanding of literature, and argued that it could play an important part in the formation of a revolutionary working class. The ensuing debate focused on three related questions. These were whether literature should be taught at all, how it should be taught, and its relationship to historical materialism. At least two contemporary developments converged on this debate: the publication in 1921 of the Newbolt Report on *The Teaching of English in England* and the discussions in Europe and the Soviet Union of the relations between literature and revolution, discussions to which Lukács and Trotsky made important contributions and which were provided with an initial sharp focus by Soviet *proletcult*. A few important articles from this debate were reported in *The Plebs*, which itself argued for a cultural dimension to political activity and for the development of working-class culture, in terms not far removed from Trotsky's *Literature and Revolution*:

> What is the lesson for us in Britain? Surely that we must not dissipate our energies; that working-class resources are not large enough to enable us successfully to deal before the revolution with culture in all its branches, irrespective of their respective importance; that our task is to provide a fighting culture for a fighting class, knowing that in any case it must remain the core of proletarian culture for a considerable period after the revolution. Let us see what Plebs have to say on the subject. I have, it will be noticed, entirely left aside for the moment the question of how far and in what way we can consciously and deliberately create proletarian art, proletarian literature, proletarian poetry and so on.
>
> (*The Plebs*, 14, 2 (1922), p. 41)

The need for a vigorous socialist and working-class literature became for a short period an important theme of the articles and reviews in *The Plebs*. The issue of working-class culture was raised most directly in a series of Soviet articles on proletarian and revolutionary culture which appeared in the paper in 1920–1. In one of these, Lunacharsky, the Bolshevik Commissar for Education and Culture, argued the importance of developing a proletarian culture before the revolution, however difficult this might be. To create this culture, the workers must read and re-evaluate bourgeois literature; and in forging their own culture they must not expect the aesthetic fullness and perfection of bourgeois art, but must judge its value first and foremost by its political effectivity, its power to mobilize class-conscious masses. But these ideas, familiar enough in the continental and Eastern European labour movements, never became established on the left in Britain, which remained attached to traditional bourgeois categories like 'realism', with all the ideological luggage that they bring in their train.

During these years a number of middle-class socialist novelists were frequently recommended to the readers of *The Plebs*, writers like Ernst Toller and Upton Sinclair; and the magazine called for British examples of the same kind of writing: moving and convincing representations of working-class life informed by a socialist warmth and vision – for a British socialist popular literature. As for existing British socialist and working-class fiction, this tended to be less enthusiastically received. For example, James Welsh's novel about Scots miners, *The Morlocks* (1924), was described as 'deficient in art', insufficiently 'vivid' and politically misguided, providing as it did negative and contradictory descriptions of working-class life. The paper also reprinted from *Izvestia* a hostile review of another of Welsh's novels, *The Underworld*, which was attacked for its 'spirit of the old, strong liberal trade unionism' and contrasted unfavourably with Harold Heslop's *The Wilderness of Toil* (published in Britain in 1934 under the title *Goaf*). The difference between the two writers was identified as a difference of political perspective. Heslop presented the solution to his characters' problems as lying in communism, and the reviewer concluded:

> That is why his book shows strong and militant spirits, where in Welsh's book we see lyricism leading often to sentimentalism. Heslop grasps the subject in a wider spirit and sees deeper into the problems with which he deals.
>
> (*The Plebs*, 18, 12 (1926), p. 449)

When Heslop's *The Gate of a Strange Field* appeared in 1929, however, it came in too for adverse comment, being described as 'not too truthful' and as 'cynical'. Once again a reading of the text's politics lay at the heart of the criticism. The reviewer objected to the often negative depiction of miners, trade unions and (not surprising, perhaps ) NCLC classes. In addition to these heresies, and in spite of some convincing writing about the colliery, the novel's failures of realism were condemned: 'It is a great pity that the two or three wonderful descriptions should lie between covers with some two hundred pages of half-baked, silly mush' (*The Plebs*, 21, 9 (1929), p. 214).

Soon after this, however, *The Plebs*, in an attempt to distance itself from the sectarianism of this kind of reviewing, moved away from the identification of literary quality with political orthodoxy; and this anti-sectarianism was also in evidence in its treatment of German communist proletarian writing.

Some of the paper's contributors had always insisted on the political value of literature.

> We want novels as well as textbooks. I've sold six *Ragged Trousered Philanthropists* for every one Plebs textbook. We shall never get at the majority of chaps with textbooks, and if our education aims at making folks class conscious, then we've got to come off all 'high-and-mightiness' and make use of every weapon which will help.
>
> (*The Plebs*, 16, 10 (1924), p. 407)

*The Plebs* in its turn acknowledged that by disregarding literature it was limiting the scope of its appeal and abandoning a whole area to the WEA – something it would not dream of doing in the case of economic or social analysis. But the recurrence, in correspondence to *The Plebs* advocating the importance of literature, of traditional idealism about the beauty of poetry putting the reader in touch with the eternal stream of life, pointed to the scale of the task, and to some extent justifies the decision to concentrate the movement's energies elsewhere.

On one occasion, in answer to readers' requests, the paper did publish a model syllabus for a literature course. This included lectures on the place of literature in independent working-class education, on historical materialism and art, on literature and the spirit of its age, the middle class and literature, and contemporary tendencies in literature. The focus here is on the relation of literature to its social and historical context. The syllabus does not raise the question of proletarian literature.

By the end of 1925, it was agreed in the pages of *The Plebs* that while courses on literature were welcome they should not have a major claim on resources. As far as the teaching of English was concerned, literacy was to be the main focus of attention for the remainder of the inter-war period, though the paper continued to carry general articles on literary topics, as well as reviews of fiction and criticism. In the thirties, as has already been noted, reviewers employed literary rather than political criteria of judgement; but, even when judged aesthetically unsuccessful, novels were often recommended to the readers of *The Plebs* on the grounds that they dealt with working-class life, and readers were encouraged to order such novels from their local library. So, while working-class writers were given little detailed or constructive attention in the Labour College movement as a whole, the importance which *The Plebs* accorded, intermittently at least, to the development of a Marxist understanding of literature and of socialist fiction on the American and continental model helped to create an interest in and a readership for working-class writing.

## International influences on the development of a left literary culture

As has been mentioned above, during the 1920s a number of reports on cultural developments in the Soviet Union were published in *The Plebs* and other left-wing papers, and stimulated some debate in this country. Interest in these matters was much greater in Europe and the USA, and reports of developments there also found their way into the left press. The Moscow-based International Bureau of Revolutionary Literature co-ordinated a number of the active national associations, the most active being the German. No such organization existed in Britain, where working-class writers were left largely to their own resources. This lack of organization helped to ensure that working-class writers remained dependent on capitalist publishers, over whom they had no control and whose decisions and assumptions they were not in a position to challenge. It was not until 1934 that a British section of what had by then become the Writers' International was formed in Britain. The founding of this section was the culmination of a process set in motion by the second International Conference of Proletarian and Revolutionary Writers, held at Charkov in November 1930. The same conference also launched the international magazine *Literature of World Revolution*.

The 1930 conference was attended by a delegation from Britain which included the miner-novelist Harold Heslop and the South Welsh miner Bob Ellis. The proceedings were heavily dominated by the political sectarianism of the Comintern's second, 'social fascist' phase, and they convey a clear idea of the impact of this policy on the cultural-political climate of the period, and of the policy changes that would be necessary to enable the founding of a non-sectarian British section of the Writers' International in 1934. In his address to the conference, Heslop gave an account of the state of bourgeois and proletarian literature in Britain. Bourgeois writing, he reported, was 'the literature of a dead people', and had 'reached a level of rottenness which can only be described as positively nauseating'. There was, however, some potential for the mobilization of bourgeois writers, some of whom were motivated by 'a revolt against the decay of capitalism'. 'Such writers could be guided by a British Section of the International Bureau of Revolutionary Literature into a clear proletarian channel' (*Literature of World Revolution*, 2 (1931), p. 226). As for working-class writing in Britain, that was, in Heslop's view, 'very backward'. He commented negatively on the work of other working-class novelists like James Welsh, John Clarke and Joe Corrie, asserting that they had 'sold out to the capitalist class' and that they 'lacked any degree of Marxist training'. He accused Welsh in particular of writing 'social fascist' novels, though he did concede too the power of censorship, and the real restrictions placed on authors by publishers. He also accused the left-wing press of failing to support working-class authors, remarking that 'during the five years of life of the proletarian newspaper – the *Sunday Worker* – the scarcity of short stories from the pens of proletarians was most pronounced'. And the difficulty of getting into print was also stressed by Bob Ellis, who welcomed the new magazine as a forum for communist and proletarian literature.

The first issue of *Literature of World Revolution* appeared in 1931. In the following year it changed to *International Literature*, under which name it lasted from 1932 till 1945 as the organ of the Writers' International, following the supersession of the Russian Association of Proletarian Writers by the Union of Soviet Writers, and the accompanying about-turn in Soviet cultural policy. Writers of various nationalities and shades of left-wing opinion contributed to the magazine, which not surprisingly contained a substantial Soviet section, dominated by the official literary doctrine of socialist realism. In these years it established itself as a forum for a range of socialist and anti-fascist writing, including fiction, literary criticism and aesthetics. The magazine helped to prepare the ground and create the constituency for the launching of the *Left Review* in 1934.

## The Writers' International and the *Left Review*

Until the founding of the British section of the Writers' International, and the contemporary development of the parallel Artists' International and of the Left Theatre movement, cultural politics had occupied only a subsidiary position on the agenda of the left and the labour movement in Britain. But from 1934 onwards this position was transformed. The *Left Review*, the official journal of the British section, made a major contribution to the politicization of culture and the broadening of the scope of political debate – as did the Left Theatre movement and from 1936 onwards the Left Book Club. The Left Book Club, in particular, organized readers' discussion groups and summer schools, and thereby extended discussion to a larger working-class and lower-middle-class audience.

The success of these developments had a good deal to do with the influence and money of a new generation of Oxford and Cambridge intellectuals who had been politicized at university and drawn into active politics by the anti-establishment and anti-fascist character of the Popular Front. One effect of their interest was to make available private money of a kind that the labour movement had not previously had access to. The *Left Review*, for example, was launched on a donation of private capital, and the people who worked on it did so without payment. Only the distribution was on a properly commercial basis. These middle-class recruits also helped to open the doors of publishing houses to radical writing, for which there was a growing market; and this in turn increased the chances of a working-class writer finding a publisher.

The *Left Review* was founded in October 1934 as a monthly forum for the exploration of questions about the social responsibility of the writer and the relationship between literature and society. It published the work of new writers with a socialist perspective, including foreign ones, as well as working-class writing – usually two or three pieces of prose and a similar number of poems in each issue. It provided a comprehensive review of left-wing publications, fiction and non-fiction, and carried features and reports on poverty, strikes, the position of women, the campaign against Mosley's fascists, the civil war in Spain and much else of the same kind, and advertised socialist organizations and events, including adult education classes.

As the organ of the Writers' International, the *Left Review* was consciously aimed at two constituencies, middle-class socialists, and working-class writers who 'desire to express in their work more effectively than in the past the struggles of their class' (*Left Review*, 1, 1 (1934), p. 38). In its first six issues, the *Left Review* published a discussion about literature and society which extended to the question of working-class writing. The central question in the debate was the meaning of commitment. Many sympathetic but unaffiliated contributors were worried about the preservation of their 'freedom' as writers, which they saw as threatened by a proletarian revolution. More controversy was generated by the suggested need to ask who writers were writing for, and to make a priority of working-class readers, providing them with constructive revolutionary literature in cheap editions. To achieve this, it was argued, middle-class writers would need direct contact with working people, and a permanent propaganda committee would be necessary to supervise the proletarianization of their outlook (Alec Brown, *Left Review*, 1, 3 (1934)). The majority of the contributors, however, subscribed to a traditional conception of intellectual freedom, with its basis in the separation of literature and politics – an idea shared by working-class and middle-class contributors alike.

In the course of this debate, C. Day Lewis called for a new conception of literature, raising once again the question of the relationship between literature and propaganda so controversially broached already by Alec Brown. Progressive literature should 'give an insight into the causes of events imaginatively through the reaction of society on the individual' (*Left Review*, 1, 4 (1935), p. 129). Drawing on implicitly realist criteria, Day Lewis suggested that proletarian literature suffered from lifelessness, and needed to project individuals not just as lay figures, inertly expressive of political ideas, but as living agents and instruments of political forces. This position, unlike Brown's call for an alternative to mass popular fiction for working-class readers, attracted a good deal of support. But, while an intellectual with a leaning towards a *Scrutiny* position could in principle support this proposition, the question of what this new fiction would look like and where it would come from was another matter, and was left unresolved.

The sixth issue announced the end of the discussion phase, and called for a redrafting of the initial statement of aims and a concerted attempt to implement them. In effect, the valuable exploration of real differences of approach to the question of culture and politics, middle-class or working-class literature, was submerged in an attempt to create a kind of united front at the cultural level. The same editorial suggested the abolition of the sharp distinction between 'writers' and 'worker-writers', and called for a more sophisticated account of the totality of contemporary literature, with an acknowledgement of its anti-capitalist tendency. This marks a shift away from the more directly political and class-based terms that had provided the dominant critical mode in the twenties and early thirties, and the opening of a space, alongside Marxists directly involved in politics, for sympathetic and fellow-travelling writers not engaged in political or industrial activity but interested in the politics of literature and the literature of politics. Such limited involvement was now welcomed as a contribution to the broad cultural-political campaign. It was agreed that the left should no longer underestimate the political importance of literature in the working-class movement, and should work to develop a Marxist theory of literature and so make up for forty years of missed opportunity. They should also encourage the participation of working-class writers in these objectives: 'Theoretical advance is one of the conditions of literary advance. Another condition is knowledge of the ordinary world of people and of things, the world of work, the world of everyday economic struggle' (*Left Review*, 1, 9 (1935), p. 364).

It was to encourage working-class writing by both men and women that the *Left Review* regularly published fiction and reportage about unemployment, manual work, poverty and similar subjects. Such fiction was realist in style, often with a strongly documentary flavour. Writing of this sort was also promoted through literary competitions designed to discover new writers and to improve their work. The idea of a competition was floated in the first issue as a response to left-wing 'jargon', with the editor, Amabel Williams-Ellis, suggesting that ordinary working people did not respond to catchphrases like 'mass struggle', 'deviation' and 'ideology', and that writers needed to develop new forms of language.

The first competition invited entrants to describe an eviction, and some of the entries were printed in the third issue, with comments and some rather condescending encouragement. The comments avoid detailed commentary, and call in broad terms for the kind of realism that permits a sympathetic identification on the reader's part: 'Remember that it is the heart of this whole business to make the reader feel as if he or she were really there. Remember it is the unexpected but correct word that does the trick' (*Left Review*, 1, 3 (1934), p. 74). Competitions were held regularly, and were reported to be attracting 'plenty of entries', of which between a third and a half were from women. Topics included 'an hour or a shift at work', 'an encounter', 'strike' and 'schooldays'. Comments on the third competition included the claim that the published entries were much enjoyed by novelists, and that the editors had received enthusiastic letters about them from readers and contributors: 'Many people are watching our competition. A well-known publisher has written to one of those whose entry was published in the last issue' (*Left Review*, 1, 7 (1935), p. 177). This form of publicity was important to aspiring working-class writers, but the *Left Review* was not able to offer them much more than moral encouragement. Apart from the prizes awarded for the successful competition entries, it did not pay its contributors.

The last competition was announced in April 1937, and the guidelines give an implicit indication of the editors' expectations. Contributions were to be structured around four questions aimed at extending realistic writing to enable it to provide an authentic personal and political perspective on how the circumstances of the writer's life could be changed, and on the immediate forces opposing such a change.

In addition to the competitions, the *Left Review* also published excerpts from still-uncompleted working-class novels, including work by James Hanley, Simon Blumenfeld and Lewis Jones. In June 1936 it carried a special editorial on workers' writing, which remarked on its increase and identified the cause as political:

> This creative upsurge, this rapidly growing desire for and power of expression by the workers, is not due to the grudging facilities for higher education offered by a government which finds this one of its means for alienating the intellectual proletarian from his class. It is due to the rising tide of class consciousness and it is a direct reflection of the growing intensity of the political struggle.
>
> (*Left Review*, 2, 9 (1936), p. 417)

The full reasons for this upsurge of working-class creativity were more complex, and included the influence of adult education, the state of publishing and the development of the kind of cultural politics pursued by the *Left Review* itself. In October 1936 it carried an advertisement asking for material for a special number on the working-class writing of the previous two years; but this never materialized, for reasons that were not disclosed.

The increasing interest of publishers in working-class writing can also be seen from advertisements in the *Left Review*. In December 1936 James Hanley advertised for short stories for a collection planned by Methuen, and in October of the same year Gollancz announced a competition for 'the best genuinely proletarian novel by a British writer', with a prize of £250 in advance royalties.

The *Left Review* published notices of working-class fiction, though, like *The Plebs* and *The Highway*, infrequently. These reviews tended to look for realism of a prescriptive and 'positive' kind, as in the criticism of Walter Greenwood's *His Worship the Mayor* for its lack of any 'suggestion of a solution to the state of vulgar bigotry and exploitation on the one hand and of unrelieved want on the other' (*Left Review*, 1, 2 (1934), p. 46). Underpinning such comments, and indeed the whole *Left Review* stance on proletarian literature, was the implicit assumption that working-class experience was in itself potentially revolutionary, and that it needed only to be adequately represented for that potential to reveal itself. Realism, successfully achieved, would lead to socialism.

During the thirties, following the winning of full female suffrage in 1928, there was a growing recognition among women of the limitations of social and legislative reforms like the vote and limited access to the professions. Much of this dissatisfaction with what had been achieved in the previous decade came from women on the left, who were aware of the class-bound nature of many of these improvements in women's situation and prospects. This was the perspective represented in the *Left Review*, and it was reinforced by articles and stories written by working-class women.

The *Left Review* carried a number of reviews of books on the position of women in Britain and the Soviet Union, raising questions about the limits of 'emancipation' by setting it in a class perspective and differentiating between middle-class and working-class women. The connection between the exploitation of women and the structure of capitalist relations of production was a recurrent theme of these pieces, and the women who discussed it also questioned the desirability of the family, which, they suggested, had been unaffected by recent changes in the legal and occupational status of women: 'The family as an economic unit remained unassailable and the double exploitation of working women continued unchanged' (*Left Review*, 1, 12 (1935), p. 500). The same piece noted that discriminatory pay was still widespread, and that working-class women were as shackled as ever. Other articles discussed birth control, childcare and abortion.

Short stories and autobiographical sketches by women included descriptions of the effects of poverty and unemployment on women as wives and mothers, the burden of repeated pregnancies and working conditions for women. One such piece interestingly contrasted books for women in a works library – exclusively popular romances – with the reading available in a library organized by the workers: not only a different kind of reading, but the same kind for men and women.

## *New Writing* and working-class fiction

The other main forum for working-class writing was John Lehmann's magazine *New Writing*, launched, like much else, in 1936 and published in six-monthly bound volumes. Lehmann argued that there was a need in Britain for a literary magazine for people with a common political opposition to fascism and war, a kind of left-wing alternative to T. S. Eliot's High Tory *Criterion*. In contrast to the *Left Review, New Writing* set out to be first and foremost literary, publishing the work of left-wing novelists and poets, translations of foreign fiction, and the work of writers who started without any of the advantages of middle-class education (Lehmann's phrase) but could write with firsthand knowledge of coal-mines, ships and factories.

The fiction published in *New Writing* was realistic in style and subject-matter. In addition to short stories, Lehmann also published extracts from novels which would have been unlikely otherwise to attract the financial assistance necessary for completion. Ralph Bates, Leslie Halward and James Hanley were among the working-class authors who found publishers in this way.

## Conclusion

This chapter offers a necessarily partial picture of the cultural-political context of working-class writing in the inter-war period. None the less, it does begin to define how far and in which ways it was possible to conceptualize and develop a radical, class-conscious, socialist literature. It remains for us to draw together the main factors which constituted this cultural-political context and to consider them in relation to the situation today.

From the brief account given above, it can be seen that conceptions of literature and working-class writing varied considerably in working-class education and socialist cultural politics. The range of available positions included the assumption, fundamental to liberal-humanist discourse, that literature transcends everyday life and is concerned with universal human values. Also encompassed was the belief, widely held by non-Marxist socialists, that literature is a direct expression of everyday life and, as such, a guarantor of the need for social reform. In its most radical, Marxist formulation, literature was seen as a tool in the formation of a revolutionary socialist consciousness.

For most readers, writers and critics, literature had the ostensibly non-political function of forming the intellectual and moral character of the individual. In the dominant discourses of the period, the individual was assumed to be a unique, ungendered, unclassed subject. The denial of the effectivity of socially produced structures of class and gender difference in the constitution of individual subjects was an essential part of the ideological project ascribed to literature, which was to produce a shared system of beliefs and values and thereby a national, ideological unity.

The formation of the moral and intellectual character of individuals was also seen as the central function of literature for much working-class adult education and cultural politics. It was a key feature of the labour-socialist tradition which accepted 'true' wisdom and morality as fixed and recognizable qualities, which transcended class difference and were the precondition for achieving, through legislation, the social transformations necessary to bring about a socialist society. It was only in Marxist discourse that literature was seen to be a historically specific, class-produced, ideological phenomenon.

The different positions on the nature of literature and its social and political functions in the inter-war period had important implications for the ways in which working-class writing was perceived. For those who held to the ideological transcendency of literature, the question of the class origin of the author was an important issue only in so far as it touched upon the aim of spreading a common culture and shared values to all. More central to this discourse was the nature of the text produced. Did it conform to or contravene the conventions whereby texts were defined as literary? Certainly, if it were overtly political, it could not be described as 'literature'. To qualify as literature it should present a realist representation of a working-class environment. It should deal with human nature as manifest in individuals in a way that did not challenge those dominant forms of ideology and morality which were seen as the substance of a humane, democratic society. In this way it could testify to the shared humanity and value of all individuals, whatever their class, and could serve socialists as a guarantee of and evidence for the justness of their cause. It was only in Marxist cultural politics, where class consciousness and struggle were emphasized, rather than displaced by universally shared standards, that working-class writing was seen to be important, in its own right, as a specific kind of literature with a directly political role to play.

Yet, while there were fundamental divergences within the labour movement on the nature and social function of literature and working-class writing, there was by the inter-war period much less apparent difference between the various positions on the question of literary form. Realism in its various definitions was espoused by all.

The unspoken dilemma for working-class writers of the inter-war years was how to make the reader and critic believe in the objectivity and therefore 'truth' of the text. In a climate in which non-Marxist literary discourse insisted on the total separation of art and politics, the objectivity of the text was predicated on its lack of overt politics. In effect, success meant conformity to conventions of realism which assumed that literature transcended specific class interests and was concerned with truth and with the individual and universal human values which guaranteed a humane society. Again it was only in some forms of Marxist criticism – seen, for example, in *The Plebs* and the *Left Review* – that alternative standards for judging literary success were developed. These shifted the boundaries of the literary and the relationship between literature and propaganda.

The dominance within the labour movement of cultural-political discourses that linked literature with personal development, placing it outside the political sphere, had implications for the material infrastructure necessary to support radical cultural production. It remained virtually nonexistent, and working-class writers were placed as isolated individuals, attempting to achieve success within the framework of a capitalist publishing industry. Nor did the labour movement do much to promote a readership for the writing which was published. It is clear that the priority given to economics and history by the trade unions and political parties was an important factor here. While this is understandable in the inter-war period, particularly in the light of the Marxism of the time, it is a factor which needs to be taken into account by alternative literary production now.

Yet, if radical cultural politics were not central to the concerns of organized labour or the left-wing intelligentsia in the inter-war period, cultural-political developments were none the less impressive. In particular, we would point to the level of engagement of working-class men and women in radical education, achievements of Marxist critics of the 1930s, and the beginning of a recognition of the significance and potential of radical fiction. Much of this momentum was lost in the war and post-war years, and it is only recently that cultural politics has reassumed a place on the agenda of the left. The reawakening of concern in issues like working-class writing has created an interest in the achievements of the past which this chapter has outlined briefly. Their implications for the present will be taken up again and discussed in the conclusion to this book.

# 4
# Gender and genre: men's stories

In the two chapters that follow, we are concerned with two issues still largely ignored by mainstream literary analysis, and with the relations between them. The first is formulaic popular fiction. The second is gender, and in particular the ways in which ideas of sexually differentiated character and function cut – deeply, if often invisibly – across the literary and cultural field. Although the discussion here is confined to novels, the generic and ideological implications are not limited to extended narratives or circumscribed by the medium of the printed book. The patterns and motifs that we analyse can be found – differently produced and inflected, certainly – in films, musicals, comic strips, magazine stories and stage plays. Walter Benjamin's essay 'The Storyteller' (Benjamin 1973) is helpful in suggesting a way of understanding this aspect of popular narratives.

Benjamin draws a distinction between the *novel*, a bourgeois form generically associated with the printed book, and the *story*, a narrative that owes less to a particular technology of literary production than to the formulaic elements of popular culture and consciousness. A story is composed of already familiar, easily recognized elements, and serves as a means of popular education, often in a highly didactic way, pointing a moral while rehearsing a tale. Both the genres considered in these chapters are closer to 'stories', in Benjamin's sense, than to novels, and the use of the term 'romance' to cover both is in part an attempt to indicate, across often considerable differences of gender, mood and plot, this common quality.

The genre of 'romance' is, in its historical origins, didactic, aristocratic and predominantly masculine. All three elements are clearly indicated, for example, in the avowed aim of Spenser's *Faerie Queene*: 'to fashion a gentleman or noble person in virtuous and gentle discipline'.[16] Yet romance nowadays is widely dismissed as trivial, lowbrow and written and read largely by women: the contemporary version of George Eliot's 'silly novels by lady novelists'. From a certain high-cultural point of view, this shift in the meaning of the word can be taken as evidence of cultural decline, of the degeneration of a high Renaissance mode, to be attributed not to the incompetence of present-day Sidneys and Spensers but to organic changes in literacy, literary culture and the relations between fiction and the reading public.

The deprecation of modern romance as a degenerate form derives its terms and assumptions from a literary ideology whose role in producing standards of taste and judgement, and their wider social equivalents, was discussed in Chapter 2. The popularization and feminization of romance – the first of these already in train in the seventeenth century, but both processes much more sharply visible in the later nineteenth – can be seen in part as an effect of its double exclusion by the dominant literary ideology of realism. Q. D. Leavis, for example, dubbed Dorthy L. Sayers's *Gaudy Night* 'a vicious presentation because it is popular and romantic while pretending to realism'.[17] In judgements of this kind – and they are common enough – questions of literary quality and value reveal themselves as an aspect of literary politics.

In Sidney, Spenser and Milton, the virtuous self-discipline of romantic matrimony and the private sphere of the nuclear household are offered as a liberating antithesis to the artificialities of courtly adultery and the miseries of enforced marriage. That antithesis was active in reformulating conceptions of gender, marriage and domestic responsibility in the cultural revolution of the seventeenth century, and it is preserved still in contemporary romance by its characteristic juxtaposition of love and money, heroine and 'other woman'. But the feminization of romance needs also to be seen against the parallel history of *feminism*. If domestic security, femininity and the holiness of the heart's affections represent, for infant capitalism, the ideological cornerstones of an emergent bourgeois 'liberty', they are no longer able to do so in any simple way in a period in which large numbers of women are coming to experience marriage not as happiness and liberation from the tyrannical father but as yet another, perhaps harsher and more complete form of patriarchal subordination. Thus modern romance, so often represented as merely reflecting back the dreams and 'escapist' fantasies of its readers, is, on the contrary, engaged in crucial ideological work: to re-enact repeatedly, in shifting historical circumstances, the moral superiority and biological inevitability of the heterosexual nuclear household as the natural embodiment of romantic love.

That last sentence is, clearly, much too simple. Romances play their part, certainly, in the ideological reproduction and naturalization of femininity, family and falling-in-love. But no account of that reproduction can afford to forget that like any other social process it is charged with contradictory and antagonistic impulsions and meanings. The naturalistic common sense that romances (like all popular narratives) generically organize and transmit is, in Gramsci's words, 'fragmentary, incoherent and inconsequential', open to multiple readings, oppositions and appropriations (Gramsci 1971, p. 491).

The history of a word and a genre, then, suggests connections with the history of gender. The genre, encompassing in its classical form not only romantic love but also adventure, quest and trial, splits markedly in the last hundred years. For the specific forms of that rupture, Benjamin's essay is once again suggestive. He distinguishes two types of storyteller: the one who stayed at home, the 'resident tiller'; and the one who travelled far and wide, the 'travelling seaman'. To these correspond two types of narrative, the domestic and the exotic. By the late nineteenth century, 'romance' can still, just, mean either or both, as in the 'romance of empire' or in Rider Haggard's to our ears eccentric description of his famous romance *King Solomon's Mines* as having 'not a petticoat in the entire history'. But the pressure on the word, its accumulating association with triviality, domesticity, fantasy and petticoats, is clear from the *OED*'s long and interesting entry, where the first signs in the latter half of the nineteenth century of its present connotations can be discerned. This changing span of definition may alert us to the intimate though complex connections, in this field at least, between gender and genre.

Though the two words descend from a single etymological root (Old French *gendre*: kind, sort), the gender divisions underlying distinctions of genre have yet to be properly elucidated. In placing adventure stories and 'women's fiction' side by side here, we have no intention of suggesting some spurious kind of sexual symmetry, an 'equal but different' philosophy applied to cultural analysis. On the contrary, there is a striking inequality in the social and literary status of the two genres. From T. S. Eliot's praise for Wilkie Collins's *The Moonstone* to the current critical vogue for the spy thrillers of John Le Carré, 'masculine romance' has enjoyed a virtual monopoly of serious attention.[18] The novels of John Buchan still appear from school stock cupboards to supply material for English lessons; and the *New Cambridge Bibliography of English Literature* gives generous representation to him, as well as to Rider Haggard and 'Sapper', while conceding none at all to Ethel M. Dell or Barbara Cartland. Nor is the writer's sex the major determination here. Agatha Christie and (Queenie Leavis notwithstanding) Dorothy L. Sayers, working in the 'masculine' genre of the detective story, fall within the ambit of 'literature', whose doors remain firmly closed to their 'romantic' sisters.

Neither is the gendering of popular genres simply a question of sexually differentiated readerships, important though that is, For it is, of course, significant that men read certain types of 'male' fiction – not least pornography – and that women read certain types of 'female' fiction, more or less exclusively. But it is also the case that women read thrillers. In doing so, however, they are inevitably involved in an act of self-alienation, since the only way in which women can have access to popular codes of knowledge, endurance, physical and intellectual agility in these forms is through the mediating codes of masculinity. 'Man' must be read, with enormous and implausible strain, as denoting 'woman' too. Love stories, on the other hand, have a virtually closed female readership. In a patriarchal linguistic order, where 'man' means human and 'woman' something less, there is not likely to be much desire or need on the part of men to enter the diminished popular codes of romance. Indeed, a man who regularly read the novels of Barbara Cartland for pleasure would be likely to find himself the object of pity, derision or clinical curiosity.

These asymmetries point to the dominance, universality and taken-for-granted character of masculinity. For this reason, literary analysis has paid little attention to the specific cultural codes of the masculine. Literature is literature, writers are writers (unless, of course, they happen to be women writers), and that is all there is to be said on the matter. Who on earth ever bothered to call Shakespeare a 'male playwright', Dickens a 'man novelist'? Only in recent years have feminist critics begun to expose and explore the inequalities that lurk within the normative pretensions of the word 'mankind'.

*

> Nowadays all the cocks are cackling and pretending to lay eggs, and all the hens are crowing and pretending to call the sun out of bed. If women today are cocksure, men are hensure. Men are timid, tremulous, rather soft and submissive. . . . And it is this that makes the cocksureness of women so dangerous, so devastating. It is really out of scheme, it is not in relation to the rest of things. So we have the tragedy of cocksure women. They find, so often, that instead of having laid an egg, they have laid a vote, or an empty ink-bottle, or some other absolutely unhatchable object, which means nothing to them.
>
> (Lawrence 1950, p. 33)

> Tilly Masterson was one of those girls whose hormones had got mixed up. He knew the type well and thought that they and their male counterparts were a direct consequence of giving votes to women and 'sex equality'. As a result of fifty years of emancipation, feminine qualities were dying out or being transferred to the males. Pansies of both sexes were everywhere, not yet completely homosexual, but confused, not knowing what they were. The result was a herd of unhappy sexual misfits – barren and full of frustrations, the women wanting to dominate and the men wanting to be nannied. He was sorry for them, but he had no time for them.
>
> (Fleming 1959, p. 269)

It would not be difficult, noting the persistence, in remarkably similar terms, of sentiments of this kind from Lawrence to Fleming, to relate them to the argument advanced by Kate Millett that a cultural counter-revolution was mobilized, after the achievement of suffrage, around sexuality and gender. Millett has shown how the romantic humanism of Lawrence, Miller and Mailer represents a very specifically *masculine* reaction to feminism and to contemporary discourses of gender and sexuality, an ideological counter-offensive designed to hold or regain ground threatened by 'fifty years of emancipation'. The differences between the two passages, and others in the same vein, might help to give some substance to the truism that masculinity, like all other elements of a hegemonic order, is not static but has constantly to adapt and manœuvre in order to secure its dominance. The second passage could also stand as a clear example of the instructive character of popular fiction, and, more formally, of the particular ideological effect of free indirect speech within a broadly realist narrative mode in naturalizing opinions and values as self-evident matters of common sense and general agreement.

But all this would still tell us next to nothing about how and why it *works*, if it does, at different times and for different readers, nor about how those opinions and values are realized and contextualized in the narrative. For example, how is it possible (as it certainly is) for a male reader openly to recognize and reject the absurdity and tendentiousness of this kind of textual buttonholing (for Fleming/Bond is the classic saloon-bar bore), and yet to be pleasurably and responsively held by a story which is effectively saying the same thing in a different way? 'Willing suspension of disbelief' won't do, not least because the reader's assent is being solicited not for some extravagant flight of fantastic invention but for the deep ideological grain and substance of the dominant culture. Nor is it plausible to suggest that we can somehow read the story while ignoring or refusing its ideological persuasions, since the latter structure the conditions of intelligibility of the former.

For example, the authority of the hero is typically registered at the outset, in masculine romance, in terms of an explicit and normative heterosexuality. This might seem so obvious as not to be worth saying. But an interesting feature of the genre is that, in spite of an overwhelming presumption to the same effect, it seems compelled, with sometimes pettish insistence, to repeat the fact. Women's romances don't seem to feel the need constantly to reassure their readers that the heroine is sexually 'normal'. Is this because she is the object rather than the initiating subject of the sexual discourse? Or because the sphere of domestic femininity constitutes her whole world, her *raison d'être*? Whereas the protagonist of the thriller or adventure story has another world, of male camaraderie, rivalry and contest, whose ambiguous and potentially unstable values and connotations need to be neutralized by ritual reassurances of sexual conformity?

This feature of masculine romance is the more noticeable for being generally incidental and inorganic to the narrative proper; another contrast with feminine romance, where the discourse of gender, of regulated heterosexual monogamy, is pivotal. It may take the form of a discursive aside:

> This was just what he had been afraid of. These blithering women who thought they could do a man's work. Why the hell couldn't they stay at home and mind their pots and pans and stick to their frocks and gossip and leave men's work to the men?
>
> (Fleming 1953, p. 123)

Or it may occur casually, as part of the initial *mise-en-scène*, a transient encounter that serves to establish the authority of the hero's 'point of view', his command of visual and ideological space, his sexual connoisseurship:

> I stepped forward to the desk and said, 'Rearden – to see Mr Mackintosh.'
>
> The red-headed girl behind the desk favoured me with a warm smile and put down the tea-cup she was holding. 'He's expecting you,' she said. 'I'll see if he's free.' She went into the inner office, closing the door carefully behind her. She had good legs.
>
> (Bagley 1973, p. 5)

> O'Hara was just leaving when he paused at the door and turned back to look at the sprawling figure in the bed. The sheet had slipped revealing dark breasts tipped a darker

> colour. He looked at her critically. Her olive skin had an underlying coppery sheen and he thought there was a sizeable admixture of Indian in this one. With a rueful grimace he took a thin wallet from the inside pocket of his leather jacket, extracted two notes and tossed them on the bedside table. Then he went out, closing the door quietly behind him.
>
> (Bagley 1967, p. 7)

> Her legs were long, rather thin, and covered with golden sand broken by zigzag trickles of water. For some reason I like watching a girl's legs covered with sand; psychologists probably have a long word for it. I have a short one.
>
> (Lyall 1967, p. 38)

Peripheral though they may seem to the story, passages of this kind can be understood in relation, on the one hand, to a wider set of readerly expectations, an intricate meshing of sexual and literary ideologies perhaps specific to the reading of popular fiction; and, on the other, to the hero's very noticeable interest in other *men*, an interest documented in far greater detail and suggestive of an elaborate underlying typology of masculine attributes and a continuous process of comparative evaluation, of 'sizing up'.

> He was a sand-coloured man with light gingery hair and invisible eyebrows and eyelashes which gave his face a naked look. If he didn't shave for a week probably no one would notice. He was slight in build and I wondered how he would use himself in a rough-house.
>
> (Bagley 1973, p. 6)

> O'Hara grunted. He did not like Grivas, neither as a man nor as a pilot. He distrusted his smoothness, the slick patina of pseudo good breeding that covered him like a sheen from his patent leather hair and trim toothbrush moustache to his highly polished shoes.
>
> (Bagley 1967, p. 9)

> He hadn't changed much. Broad, stocky, steady, like the hand. A snub square face with a tanned and oddly coarse skin, pale blue eyes, short curly fair hair.
>
> (Lyall 1967, p. 16)

In each of these, unlike the superficially similar observations of women, which are generally quite inconsequential for the story, there is a significant anticipation of narrative, an intuition about 'character' of almost allegorical formality. We know straight away that one man will be clever, evasive, ambiguous, another slimily treacherous, and so on. To these adjectival codes of appearance could be added the adverbial codes of action: moved swiftly, looked up sharply, and the like. At each stage, through fine adjustments of comparison, contrast, rivalry and degrees of approval, the hero's own definition as a man becomes sharper, without ever being explicitly presented as such.

The elusiveness and ambiguity of the protagonist, the need for constant textual activity to test and reaffirm his status, the frequent absence of strong narrative closure – all characteristics in which masculine romance differs markedly from its feminine counterpart – might seem to suggest that ideologies of masculinity are less securely grounded, less assured than those of femininity. But this is surely not the case. Indeed, it may be that the apparent insecurity is itself a powerful form of masculinity, an overarching level of textual ideology characteristic of the genre as a whole. For, if women are 'born', men have to be 'made'. 'Being a woman' presents itself as natural, instinctual, requiring no effort, only acquiescence to a biological destiny. But 'being a man' (note the more active, strenuous tonality of the phrase) is an unceasing effort, a tense and vigilant posture of the will, ever on the alert against the terrible, the unthinkable humiliation of being unmasked, in an unguarded moment, as a cissy, a pansy or a weed. It is this correspondence between a lived ideology and a particular form of narrative, rather than any contingencies of content or readership, that makes it possible to talk of masculine romance as an axiomatically gendered genre or group of genres.

As for masculinity itself, it might be analytically more useful to talk about *masculinities*, as a way of signalling the variety of its historical and social forms. Certainly a concept that seems to lump together guards officers and skinheads in an undifferentiated solidarity might be thought to simplify a little. And yet the solidarity is there, in forms that intersect with, complicate and sometimes override other affiliations, including class. Extreme situations provide examples: fascism, for example, and war. It will not do to write such things off as mere aberrations of false consciousness, beneath which some more 'fundamental' contradiction persists unaltered. Gender is a 'relation of production', and not only of ideological and cultural production either.

The singular form also serves as a reminder of the immensely extended historical duration of patriarchal power. The 'eternal charm' of Greek art, which so puzzled Marx (Marx 1973, p. 111), must surely owe something to the persistance, across millennia of social change, of Homeric codes of male honour, bravery and cunning, of female beauty, submissiveness and treachery. And, as Gramsci recognized, it is the despised and trashy fictions of the market, working as they do with the sedimented and mythopoeic materials of popular common sense, rather than the modern 'classics' of the high-literary canon, that have the closest relation to those ancient models, those enduring myths of power.

*

The stress, in surveys of the genre, falls repeatedly on the didactic and instructional nature of popular fiction for men and boys. Patrick Howarth's *Play Up and Play the Game* (Howarth 1973) follows the heroes of boys' stories from Christian Socialism and muscular piety through Boys' Heroes and imperial adventure to the G-men and secret agents of the thirties and forties. The didacticism of such fiction is also explored in Richard Usborne's *Clubland Heroes* (Usborne 1974), where the presentation of the world of male upper-crust 'Clubland' is interpreted as a preparatory education for those young readers encouraged to read John Buchan or Geoffrey Household by fathers, uncles and schoolmasters. Closer correspondences with the public-school ethos and the old-boy network are identified by Usborne, as they are in Colin Watson's *Snobbery with Violence* (Watson 1971). Usborne in particular draws out the social ramifications of Clubland, along with 'the racism, the senseless but justified violence, the meting out of (spurious) justice to foreigners', and associates them with the actual experience of the culture of the boys' public school.

What is missing from these accounts is any recognition of the recurrent, often unstable characteristics of masculinity and its fictional representations. Roger Bromley has suggested an approach to this problem by distinguishing between masculine and feminine romance in terms of their different economies of *exchange*.

> All romance (masculine or feminine) is based on an exchange relation. Feminine romance is not about love but about marriage . . . whereas masculine romance is based on exchange at the level of mental or physical conflict (the game, etc.) between two males. . . . Both modes of exchange reduce social connectedness to the couple.
>
> (Bromley 1978, p. 43)

What is important here is Bromley's insistence on the competitiveness and gamesmanship underpinning conceptions of masculinity in fictions of this kind. In a transitional text like *Rogue Male* (Household 1939), the exchange occurs at the level not only of mental and physical conflict but also of identity and subjectivity. Indeed, this is one of the features that suggests that it can be viewed as a 'break text' or moment of transformation within the genre.

By 'masculine romance', then, we refer to those popular fictions that articulate as a dominant concern the values and codes of masculinity. In this sense the term covers an enormous range, from *Boys' Own* and *Biggles* to westerns and Bond, each with its own particularities of production, readership and mode of address. A contrast might be drawn, for example, between that group of narratives whose major reference is male solidarity and camaraderie (most westerns, war stories and school stories would fall into this category) and those that focus predominantly on personal relationships and questions of moral and sexual identity (many thrillers, detective stories, spy stories). The former are concerned principally with the world of male work and the mastery of public space, while the latter foreground the problematics of friendship, loyalty and sexuality in a corrupt and menacing world – the morally ambiguous world of the private eye, the double agent and the decent cop. One way of indicating the borderline status of *Rogue Male* would be to see it as an instance or at least a descendant of the first type (an adventure yarn in the Buchan tradition) struggling to become an example of the second (the existential thriller, in the manner of Greene or Le Carré) – a generic ambiguity that implicates the text in striking deconstructions and reconstitutions of the codes of class and masculinity.

Penguin now market *Rogue Male* as 'in a class with Ambler, Le Carré and Buchan'; and indeed the narrative recalls by turns the political thriller, the 'existential' spy story and the straightforward boy's adventure romance. The blurb summarizes the narrative as follows:

> His mission is revenge, and revenge means assassination; in return he'll be cruelly tortured by secret agents, hunted by the police, relentlessly pursued by Quive-Smith. They'll turn him into a Rogue Male, and to survive he'll have to think and live like a beast.
>
> (Household 1968)

The story takes the form of a diary confession, covering the few months from the attempted assassination of a Central European dictator (the subsequent film plumped for Hitler, but the text remains carefully ambiguous) to the anonymous aristocratic protagonist's reincarnation as an inconspicuous Central American businessman. The diary form, including the fragmentary letter to a friend with which the text closes, breaks with the traditional modes of the genre and introduces a degree of self-reflection, the adventure story being presented almost at second hand, mediated by a recurrent discourse of memory and identity.

> At present, I exist in my own time, as one does in a nightmare, forcing myself to a fanaticism of endurance. Without a God, without a love, without a hate – yet a fanatic! An embodiment of the myth of foreigners, the English gentleman, the gentle Englishman. I will not kill: to hide I am ashamed. So I endure without object.
>
> (Household 1968, pp. 128–9)

This, as we've said, is one of the features that leads us to consider *Rogue Male* a 'break text', a narrative that pushes the conventions of its genre to the limit, and in the process affords the reader a perspective backwards and forwards across the genre's historical development. *Rogue Male* is as centrally concerned with establishing, in a moment of historical and personal crisis, a feasible male identity as with narrating an adventure. Questions of masculinity are placed prominently and problematically in the foreground:

> I was magnificently fit as a result of my life in the open and the brisk autumn air. I remember how easily my muscles answered the call I made on them. By God, in all this immobility and carrion thought, it does me good to think of the man I was.
>
> (Household 1968, p. 94)

*Rogue Male* employs a number of interesting narrative devices. The hero does not name himself.

> I create a second self, a man of the past by whom the man of the present may be measured. Lest what I write should ever . . . become public property I will not mention who I am.
>
> (Household 1968, pp. 14–15)

A social past is continually referred to (country estate, club in town, professional interests, circle of social acquaintance) as a way of establishing a retrospectively secure and traditional existence from which he is now exiled. To succeed in the activity of pure male combat, that past identity and the social rituals associated with it have to be exploited. But the hero remains anonymous, the elusive tenant of a series of disguises and transient personalities. His identity fractured, we are offered instead an array of sub-identities which he occupies in his flight from hunt to permanent exile, from 'bored and wealthy Englishman' to 'Latin gentleman'. In this way the narrative explores the means by which a displaced representative of the landed gentry relocates himself in relation to the society from which he has been eliminated.

This clearly invites social and historical analysis, in terms, say, of the negotiated relations between traditional and more recently emergent fractions of the propertied classes, and of their differential relations to ideologies and economies of national (English) and transnational ('Latin') character. But our concern here is with a different though not unconnected set of ideologies: those of gender. On the way to his final social and geographical relocation, the hero retains the role of sportsman in all the rituals through which he lays claim to his new identity. But all other identifying marks have first to be cleared away.

> The next job was to see my solicitor in Lincoln's Inn Fields. . . . After lunch I signed a number of documents to tidy up loose ends, and we blocked out a plan I had often discussed with him of forming a kind of Tenants' Co-operative Society.
>
> (Household 1968, p. 57)

The assassination itself is understood by the hero as a kind of game, a sporting challenge ('who could resist the temptation to stalk the impossible?') undertaken for personal reasons, with no wider political motivation. The rituals of sport and game are combined with a scholarly knowledge of ancient weaponry as the hero, himself stalked to his foxhole by the equally sporting Major Quive-Smith, improvises a primitive crossbow out of the natural raw materials around him:

> I have been interested in the mechanics of obsolete weapons and guilty of boring my friends by maintaining the supremacy of the Roman artillery over any other up to the Napoleonic wars. The engine that I had now constructed was an extremely crude model of a hand-drawn ballista.
>
> (Household 1968, p. 162)

Reliance on such artisanal craft skills is characteristic of the classical period of the adventure thriller, and contrasts strongly with the high-technical expertise, the technological modernism, to be found in the post-war thriller. The ending of *Rogue Male* tends to confirm the intuition that the novel is, within its genre, a transitional text, for the hero finally abandons the fields and woods and the associated rural skills of his beloved Dorset and rediscovers his destiny in a new setting and a fresh identity, urban, cosmopolitan and modern:

> I began to see where I went wrong the first time. It was a mistake to make use of my skill over the sort of country I understood. One should always hunt an animal in its natural habitat; and the natural habitat of man is – in these days – in a town. Chimney pots should be the cover, and the method, snap shots at two hundred yards. My plans are far advanced.

> I shall not get away alive, but I shall not miss; and that is all that really matters any longer.
>
> (Household 1968, p. 191)

The motifs of sport, game and hunt are shifting here away from their traditional settings and connotations – rural, feudal and gentleman amateur – towards their later articulation, in the Bond novels and the American thick-ear thriller, with the code of the urban professional. Household's anonymous sportsman-assassin adumbrates, in this transformation, not only Bond and Mike Hammer but also Forsyth's unnamed 'Jackal' and the 'professionals' and 'avengers' of a dozen films and television series. Colin Watson has characterized the sporting amateur as the key type in the masculine romance of the thirties:

> Sport is the key word in the vocabulary of a whole group of authors at the time. Its emotive significance cannot be over-estimated. Epitomizing a philosophy that over the years had been built into every stratum of rulership, instruction and administration by the public school system, this one little word served for a great number of people the combined purpose of civic code and religious regulator.
>
> (Watson 1971, pp. 48–9)

It would be a mistake, of course, to suppose that this is even now a wholly superannuated notion. Even today, when the professionals of mass extermination can shroud their lethal specialisms in the smooth, antiseptic obscurity of brand names, acronyms and high-tech jargon, the C.-in-C. in the South Atlantic can still, without a trace of irony, nominate his 'man of the match' for the Falklands campaign. But in *Rogue Male* that tweedy affability is already breaking down, giving ground to a new version of masculinity in action, the professional killer (whether 'justified' by a veneer of legality or motive matters little) – a shift whose climax is to be found, perhaps, in the spate of 'exterminator' films that has appeared in recent years.

The narrator-hero of *Rogue Male* embarks on a search for a reconstituted male identity, a strategic accommodation of sexual and social power to the demands of drastically altered circumstances. To reach the point at which a new subjectivity can be composed and the displaced and transformed aristocrat can once again possess himself, a transitional period of combat and chase, a ritual of male competitive play must take place. Themes of disguise and masculinity converge at the story's climax, when the hero defeats his pursuer and assumes the enemy's identity in order to escape. The pursuer himself, Quive-Smith (in reality a foreign agent of stereotypically devilish cunning), is almost a replica of the narrator, having assumed the disguise of an English country gentleman in order to hunt the hero unobserved in his own social world. Pursued by the police of two nations, and relying on the last vestiges of aristocratic sportsmanship and knowhow, the hero finds in his opponent a replica of himself. The English country gentleman, traditional pillar of church, shire and state, paradigm of ruling-class masculinity, is hunting himself to the finish. Yet this finish marks a new beginning in the formulation of new versions of the English hero.

# 5
# Gender and genre: women's stories

> Above all, a woman's story is a love story, which means that it will appeal to women of all ages. It is absolutely imperative that the authors realize from the outset that in dealing with romance you are handling a quality or a state of mind which enters the lives of the majority of people in the world at some time or another. Individual attitudes to romance may change with age and outlook, but while it lasts in the individual's mind, that romance is real.
>
> (Britton and Collin 1960, p. 11)

> There seems little doubt that most modern romance formulas are essentially affirmations of the ideals of monogamous marriage and feminine domesticity. No doubt the coming-of-age of women's liberation will invent significantly new formulas for romance, if it does not lead to a total rejection of the formula of love triumphant.
>
> (Cawelti 1976, p. 42)

> The domestic romance myth remains the centrepiece of feminine culture. Sexual religion is the opiate of the supermenial. Romance sanctions drudgery, physical incompetence and prostitution.
>
> (Greer 1971, p. 188)

So there it is. Romance is either an eternal verity, an archetype of human experience, or a dangerous delusion. Any reading of romance, and of writing about it, immediately and continuously throws up contradictions of this kind. In the western capitalist world, at least, 'falling in love' is considered one of the most precious, unique and intimate of life's experiences. Yet countless thousands of stories retell that experience in the most conventional and formulaic way imaginable. In fact, the 'uniqueness' of the experience is itself one of the common conventions, the formulas of the genre. This only happens to you once in a lifetime, the stories tell us, over and over again.

In this chapter we are concerned with some of the structuring conventions of romantic fiction. These conventions are at one and the same time moral and aesthetic, ideological and formal. The well-behaved, monogamous and faithful end happily; the bad end badly. The stories mobilize conventions and formulas at every point, from the macro-level of the plot to the micro-level of the single sentence. Writers' handbooks like the one quoted above (Britton and Collin 1960) teach the aspiring author how many ways there are of organizing the 'boy meets girl, girl meets boy' plot; how to lead up to and describe the kiss, directly or indirectly; how to suggest character through physical detail – hot-tempered redheads, granite jaws, brooding eyes, strong fingers, and the like. What do these conventions have to do with the popularity of romance among the women who form their virtually exclusive readership?

Romance has incurred almost universal condemnation. Cultural conservatives see it as an integral part of the 'shapeless, sprawling, anti-human mass' of a debased popular culture. Much Marxist analysis mirrors this reactionary view, blaming a capitalist 'culture industry' for the destruction of working-class consciousness and the 'massification' of culture. Both these analyses are presented by Alan Swingewood in *The Myth of Mass Culture* (1977), and their connecting threads revealed.

Popular fiction has also been studied for the formulaic narrative devices it deploys. Fictional formulas which are repeated over and over again may, as John Cawelti suggests (Cawelti 1976), speak to basic human needs, with romance repeating the formula of 'love triumphant'. On the other hand, they may act, as Roger Bromley has suggested (Bromley 1978), as a systematic misrepresentation of the basic conflicts of modern capitalist societies. Thus, in Catherine Cookson's novels, heredity replaces and displaces class struggle as the motor of history.

With the exception of the argument of the cultural conservatives (for the nature of the 'anti-human' in the Leavis tradition is rarely *argued*, it is *assumed*), each of these accounts makes some sense. Mills and Boon represent one of the very few profitable sectors of British publishing nowadays: there really *are* 'profits in pulp'. At the same time, many romance formulas – like the pattern of loss and recovery – *are* found in love stories from widely different cultures and historical periods. Yet the *differences* between Barbara Cartland's *Vote for Love*, Chaucer's *Troilus and Criseyde* and Longus's *Daphnis and Chloe* are at least as striking, in narratological terms, as the similarities.

Only feminist analysis, however, has shown any serious concern (as opposed to patronizing or dismissive generalization) with the relationship between romance and the lives of women. And it takes a brave woman to state the obvious, and then go on to question it. In the early writings of the post-war women's liberation movement, writers like Germaine Greer and Shulamith Firestone presented romantic love and its fictional representations as, simply, a form of deception aimed at preventing women from recognizing and seeking to alter their subordinate position in male-dominated society. But more recently, in less optimistic mood, feminist intellectuals have been critically aware of the durability and genuine popularity of these forms.

Unless romantic fiction is seen as part of the sexual divisions of society, its conventions cannot be understood. Further, if we do not see those conventions in their relation to wider ideologies of femininity and masculinity, we shall not understand their popular appeal. The power of these fictions is directly related to their ability to represent structural features of the position of women in relation to men. And just as that position both changes *and* exhibits deeply persistent features, so too do romantic fictions show elements of change and of profound continuity.

Certainly romance formulas do change over time. In *The*

*Purple Heartthrobs* Rachel Anderson claims that 'popular romantic fiction began in 1853 with the publication of *The Heir of Redclyffe* by Charlotte M. Yonge' (Anderson 1974, p. 25) – an assertion less arbitrary than it seems, since the date marks the rendezvous of a particular kind of fiction for women, the love story with a moral purpose, and the marketing of that fiction through Mudie's Select Circulating Library. In *Heroines in Love*, a collection of women's romantic magazine fiction, Mirabel Cecil locates its origin in 1749: a similar conjuncture of a form – the story of the heroine fighting to retain her virtue – and a means of circulation, the women's magazine (Cecil 1974).

It was not, however, until the end of the nineteenth century, with the appearance of the cheap single volume, that romantic fiction finally became widely available to the mass of women. Anderson regards the period from the mid-nineteenth to the early twentieth century as the heyday of romantic fiction, with Marie Corelli, Ouida, Florence Barclay, Elinor Glyn, Ethel M. Dell and E. M. Hull as its classic authors. All these had a personal, evangelizing sense of mission on behalf of their own philosophies of life, whether against atheism and feminism or in praise of the power of love. In spite of their staunch defence of traditional values, all evoked the scorn and outrage of the literary establishment; but now they enjoy a canonical prestige and authority of their own. Denise Robbins, former president of the Romantic Novelists' Association, has claimed that no one who has not read Ouida can understand the art of romantic fiction; and Barbara Cartland – appropriately a great believer in reincarnation – has recycled her predecessors, E. M. Hull, Ethel M. Dell and Elinor Glyn, in 'Barbara Cartland's Library of Love'. Like the canon of academic literary criticism, the 'classics' of romantic fiction have been selected and composed into a 'tradition'.

Two novels from this tradition may help to suggest features of continuity and change in romance: Florence Barclay's *The Rosary* (1909) and E. M. Hull's *The Sheik* (1921), both of them bestsellers over many years.

*The Rosary* is the story of the Hon. Jane Champion and Garth

Dalmain – how she first refuses him for fear of imposing her plainness on his artist's eyes, how he is blinded, how she returns incognito from Egypt to nurse him, and how their love is finally brought to fulfilment through music and Jane's beautiful singing-voice. Barclay's stated purpose was 'never to write a line which could introduce a taint of sin or the shadow of shame into any home' (Anderson 1974, p. 131), and to communicate to her readers 'the holy power of music'. The novel is shaped by a religious dualism between soul and body, transcended by the effects of prayer and by the supernatural power of religious-erotic music. It is this religiosity, with its unequivocal representation of divine intervention in the love affair, which distances *The Rosary* most clearly from contemporary romance.

*The Sheik* was – and is still – regarded as a scandalous book. 'Diana Mayo is the first romantic heroine to be sexually assaulted, to learn during 300 pages to enjoy it, and to marry the man who did it' (Anderson 1974, p. 184). Diana Mayo, the heroine, has been brought up as a boy and while travelling through the desert, is abducted by the Sheik. When (after 300 pages) rape provokes love, the Sheik is revealed to be the son of an English lord. The explicit and repeated representation of female sexuality as masochistic, along with a racism that counterposes 'foreign' rape and brutality to the firmness of English masculinity, structures the narrative. Racism of this kind, while it has far from disappeared from contemporary romance, rarely forms a central feature of the love story nowadays.

If self-confident religious and imperialist ideologies in romantic fiction belong, for the time being, to another age, an explicit concern with masculinity and femininity does not. Both novels are about the transformation of women.

> I was brought up as a boy. My training was hard. Emotion and affection have been barred out of my life. I simply didn't know what they mean. I don't want to know. I am very content with my life as it is. Marriage for a woman means an end to independence, that is, marriage with a man who is a man, in spite of all that the most modern woman may say. I have never obeyed anyone in my life. I do not wish to try the experiment.
>
> (Hull 1921, p. 13)

(Diana ends the novel happy but 'pleading like a terrified child' (Hull 1921, p. 253).)

> Tears never came easily to Jane. But tonight she had been called a name by which she had never thought to be called; and already her honest heart was telling her she would never be called it again. And large silent tears overflowed and fell upon the lace at her breast. For the wife and mother in her had been wakened and stirred, and the deeps of her nature broke through the barriers of stern repression and almost masculine self-control, and refused to be driven back by the womanly tribute of tears.
>
> (Barclay 1909, p. 102)

Across the divisions between 'rough' and 'respectable' novels, chaste and suggestive romances, this 'melting' and 'taming' of women by men recurs. Women's necessary *obedience* to the commands of love is a continuing theme.

It is likely that some of the shifts in the formulas of romantic fiction can be related quite closely to historical and social change. Where would doctor-and-nurse romances be without the National Health Service, or imperialist adventure without the Boer War, or the exotic international settings of some recent romances without the transnationalization of capital and the advent of the package holiday? Other shifts, again, can be related to particular moments in the struggle for women's emancipation. The central stress on obedience and the disciplining of female independence has a powerful relevance to the period of feminist rebellion over suffrage, when both novels enjoyed their greatest popularity.

*

Most contemporary romances, though actually the work of individual authors, are anonymous, or known by the publisher's rather than the author's name: Mills and Boon, *My Weekly*. But those writers of romance who transcend the anonymity of the genre and become widely known in their own right often supply not only popular narratives but a whole life-philosophy, a 'theory', that goes well beyond the pages of their fiction. From the *Marie Corelli Calendar and Birthday Book*, through Elinor Glyn's *Philosophy of Love* to Denise Robbins's agony column in *She*, 'one of the ancillary activities of writing romantic novels has often been to provide advice or practical help on love and its related topics – beauty, sex, homeliness, woman's role in the home' (Anderson 1974).

Beyond the anonymous world of romantic fiction, two contemporary romantic novelists have achieved a special pre-eminence: Barbara Cartland and Catherine Cookson. Cookson's work is to a large extent a reworking of themes from her own life story. Her autobiography *Our Kate* tells how she was born illegitimate, the child of an alcoholic mother. She had no formal education, and worked 'in service' and later in a laundry, moving south to Hastings where she married a schoolteacher. *Our Kate* tells too of her experience of nervous breakdown. All her fiction has drawn on this story as 'representative experience'.

Cartland's fiction, extensive as it is, forms only one part of a broader philosophical enterprise. *The Writers' Diary* describes her as 'writer of romantic and historical novels, historical biographer, writer on health and physical fitness, and autobiographer. Freelance writer and public speaker.' According to a recent estimate she has published 267 novels and sold 120 million copies of them worldwide, in a novel-writing career that began in 1925. The production of fiction has been punctuated regularly by works of philosophy, sociology and the advocacy of honey, vitamins and health food in the pursuit of perpetual life and love. *Touch the Stars: A Clue to Happiness* (1936), *You in the Home* (1946), *The Fascinating Forties* (1954), *Vitamins for Vitality* (1959), *Sex and the Teenager* (1964), *Living Together* (1965) and *The Magic of Honey* (1970) all give practical advice to women on the arts of femininity and romantic love.

The majority of Barbara Cartland's readers are undoubtedly working class or lower middle class. But Cartland herself comes from a very different world. 'We had been brought up in a political atmosphere. Meetings, elections, speeches, pamphlets, the Primrose League – they were part of our environment. Yes, Ronald must be Prime Minister, but I must do something too' (Cartland 1942, p. 12). What she did do was become, first, a gossip-columnist for the *Daily Express*, then a novelist – a 'something' which has formed a connection for many middle-class women between the private world of the home and the public world of men. As a novelist, she became a chronicler of the world in which she had grown up, the world of Society and 'the Season', whose power and purpose have been analysed by Leonore Davidoff in *The Best Circles* (1973). Society and the Season were first formally codified in the 1820s as rituals of access to political power for the newly wealthy industrial bourgeoisie. The sites of these rituals were the great country houses of the aristocracy and gentry, their London town-houses, and the greatest private house of the grandest family of all, the Palace. Women were both the currency and the bonds of this formation, exchanged in marriage and presiding over the accompanying rituals. As Davidoff explains,

> By effectively preventing upper and middle-class women from playing any part in the market, any part in public life whatsoever, the Victorians believed that one section of the population would be able to provide a haven of stability and of exact social classification in the threatening anonymity of the surrounding economic and political upheaval.
>
> (Davidoff 1973, p. 16)

By the time Barbara Cartland herself 'came out' – and certainly by the time her first novel was published – Society's monopoly of political influence had already been challenged by the representation of labour and the success of the women's suffrage agitation, as well as by the shockwave of the First World War. But its other function, as a marriage-market for high-bourgeois and 'county' families, continued until its official dismantling in 1957, and of course persists less formally even today.

This set of social rituals provides the basis for the representation of public and private spheres in Barbara Cartland's novels. The 'power behind the throne' which Society women exercised was based on the control of their childbearing capacity and their confinement in the home. But that home was, in domestic affairs at least, controlled by women, and in the nineteenth century, when parliament was still 'the most exclusive club in town', the private house was a major factor in the exercise of political influence. In *Again This Rapture* Cynthia Morrow's knowledge of how to organize a ball for his daughter and the county is necessary to Robert Shelford. Only women can make the outsider 'belong'. The hero states:

> This house has sheltered my mother; it has made a background for the daughter of whose existence I had no idea when I first contemplated coming here. Now its usefulness is finished. I realize I am alien here. I have never belonged. It was your home and should belong to no-one else.
>
> (Cartland 1967, p. 190)

The country house is a key symbol in Cartland's writing. The grounds are lovingly described, the rooms and their furniture dotingly catalogued. And it is always central to the relationship of hero and heroine. It signifies not only the boundaries of class but also, more importantly in this genre, the boundary of masculine and feminine domains and values, of public and private spheres of life. More often than not it is the sight of the heroine in the country house that awakens the hero to her fitness to be his wife and bear his children. And it also functions to mark the heroine off from the 'city women' who recur in the books, women who transgress the boundaries of city and country, public and private, and play by the men's rules.

'City men' and 'men of the world', on the other hand, move between public and private all the time, even in 'bodice-ripper' romances. Eric Damon, international financier and hero of the Candlelight and Ecstasy romance *The Tempestuous Lovers*, owns the same kind of house as Cartland's eligible bachelors. This time it is called 'Frenchman's Court':

> You are the first 'friend' – male or female – that I have ever allowed inside my home. I come to Maine to relax, to walk through the woods, or along the beach, to swim in the nude off a private cove. This is my sanctuary. I want no association here with the outside world. Here I can be what I like. . . . There are no timetables here or schedules, no ticker tape, no television – although I think Mrs Berman has a small one in her apartment over the garage – no photographers, no reporters. Here I have privacy.
>
> (Simmons 1982, p. 131)

Catherine Cookson's 'Mallen Trilogy' ends with a declaration of love that depends on the same convention, in slightly different terms:

> As he put his mouth down on hers and drew her into him, he knew he had reached home.
>
> (Cookson 1974, p. 355)

Love is where the heart is. Home is where the heart is. Home is where women are, and where the world, power and work are absent. Marking the boundaries between public and private spheres is a key part of the process of securing female subordination. But in romance this female, domestic space, this very powerlessness and dependence are promoted to the foreground as a form of power and value and self-fulfilment.

In the school textbooks and in the standard accounts, women rarely appear as actors upon the public stage of history. The romantic novelist reinstates women and reverses the account. Here the history that men have made becomes the backdrop and women the protagonists in a drama of quite different significance. In Cartland's *Again This Rapture* the backdrop is the Second World War. It tells the story of Cynthia Morrow, a countrywoman whose war service has not healed the wounds caused when she was jilted by her childhood sweetheart. Because of her father's debts she loses her home, Birchwood, to Robert Shelford, a rootless adventurer from America. Cynthia has been decorated for her work as a nurse in India; but the war signifies for her only a stage on the journey towards love and marriage. She has attempted to heal a broken heart by throwing herself into nursing. She nurses an attempted suicide back to health and a happy marriage. She even attempts to use nursing as an escape from Robert Shelford, only to be told by the matron that she has sterner emotional tasks to face: 'My advice to you, Nurse Morrow, is to go back and face your problems with courage and with faith in yourself' (Cartland 1967, p. 138). Her experience in wartime also enables her to recognize the defective masculinity of her ex-fiancé, who 'did not know active war service', and has degenerated into a lecher and a drunk as a result. In the world of romance, history is no more than a signal that the course of personal life and love is running true.

The fully fledged historical romance provides a clearer instance of the same reversal. Here public characters (Henry VIII, Louis XIV) are revealed in their private lives as wonderful lovers, jealous husbands, brutal adulterers; and women enter 'history' once more as mistresses, wives and mothers, influencing affairs of state from the bedroom and the drawing room. This may help to explain why Mary Queen of Scots is far and away the most popular heroine of historical romance. She is there in all the history books, a genuine woman protagonist. And, more importantly, her power, tragedy and glamour come not from politics or war but from the female sphere of love – her own love affairs, thrown into sharper relief by the jealous hatred of her cold and virginal cousin Elizabeth. But, on the whole, the public world of history is not the world of women's power and purposes. The dynamic of their lives is not to be found there. This code is stated very plainly at the end of Cartland's *Vote for Love*, the story of a hapless and unwilling suffragette:

> 'You are everything that matters,' Rayburn said. 'Everything that a man wants in his home and in his personal world, which should always be private and apart from his public one. No vote, no alteration in a woman's status could make you more important than you are to me already, just by being a woman.'
>
> (Cartland 1977, p. 101)

This reversal of the common view of history, allowing the usually marginalized female sphere to dominate, is extended in Catherine Cookson's work and in other 'family sagas'. In the 'Mallen Trilogy' the history of the history books is only a signpost for the history of the family. Wars, parliaments and economic crises serve only as backcloths against which the Mallen 'curse' works itself out from generation to generation. The curse is inherited and genetic, indicated by the 'Mallen streak', a tuft of white hair found only in the men of the family. No Mallen who bears the streak will die in his bed. Only love, or the perfect woman – Miss Brigmore, 'mistress, wife, mother and teacher' – from outside the doomed circle of kinship can break the curse.

The domestic sphere of reproduction does have a different history, a different temporality, from the history of production, although it is connected with it. Though neither femininity nor patterns of kinship are 'natural' or eternal, both can *seem* so in comparison with other productive and social processes.

Romance conventions eternalize and naturalize historical processes. At the same time, as we have seen, they foreground a set of social relations normally relegated to the background – relations of kinship. In romance, the dynamic of masculinity and femininity is repeatedly exposed. It is remarkable, for example, how often the loss and recovery of the lovers is anticipated and mirrored in the hero's earlier loss of his father. Men like Eric, Robert, Lorn, the heroes of romantic fiction can become 'action men' only when their legitimacy and lineage has been clarified and their security assured by the love of a virtuous woman. Eric Damon, for instance, grew up in an orphanage.

> Someone like Eric has been forced to create a shell around himself for survival. But inside where it counts, he too can be vulnerable, unsure of himself, sensitive to rejection.
>
> (Simmons 1982, p. 158)

> 'You bastard.'
> 'You're right. I am illegitimate. And what if my child is a bastard, like his father?'
>
> (Oldfield 1983, p. 100)

> Only Cynthia could make him belong.
>
> (Cartland 1967, p. 42)

> He was no longer a Mallen flaunting his streak, finding pride in his bastardy, and through it feeling he had the right to confer condescension on even those who considered themselves his superiors – he was nothing. He was now as he had been that day in the marketplace when the Scolley brothers had laughed at him and called him a bastard.
>
> (Cookson 1973, p. 168)

This representation of history and its dynamic as a pattern of kinship extends to the representation of class, nation and race in romantic fiction. Barbara Cartland's fiction restores England as the heart of the world, and the family as the heart of England. In *Again This Rapture* Robert can offer Cynthia children and the healing of a broken heart; but Cynthia can offer him pure Englishness, a background and the anchor of respectability. In fiction at least, England still rules America.

To signify that the fires of love burn strongly but differently in all races and classes – and successfully too, if governed by the wisdom of Englishness – Cynthia intervenes in two wayward love stories in the course of the narrative, and helps them to return to true. One is the story of a working-class girl who has 'gone too far' and has attempted suicide to hide her disgrace from her boyfriend. She is rescued by Robert and Cynthia, and after instruction in the belief that love will conquer all material obstacles the lovers are reunited with the gift of a home and a small business from Robert. Micaela, Robert's illegitimate South American daughter, engages in a passionate love affair with an English rake, and through Cynthia's influence is enabled first to repent of her decision to elope with him and later, when his wife obligingly dies, to marry him. Their illicit mutual passion signals that both are on the margins of society.

> Women of the south ripen more quickly than their sisters from the northern hemisphere; but this indeed had little to do with years and months. It was a question of breeding, race and of an age-old knowledge handed down from generation to generation.
>
> (Cartland 1967, p. 39)

The sub-narratives of class and race are subordinated to the story of Robert and Cynthia. Their outcome depends on the successful pairing of hero and heroine, and together they signal the harmony of a happy ending.

*

> Another human being, before estimating your age, social standing, nationality, behaviour or intelligence, registers one vital fact: your sex. The point is so obvious that many people are inclined to forget it. Some remember, but pretend to ignore it. They talk about human beings first and foremost, with their existence as men and women as a secondary factor. When they do so they are directing their lives towards disillusion and disaster.
>
> (Cartland 1957, p. 7)

> The endless pages of tingling skins and the desire to bruise the mouth have never been described as porn. But that's really what they are. Yet I've seen no-one marching in the street to ban the neo-Gothic novel.
>
> (English 1982, p. 47)

There is a clear and strong sexual division in the industry and conventions of sexual fantasy: romance for women, pornography for men. Some, though not all, romances are sexually explicit; but all depend on the structuring and repetition of thrills of delight. Inside a private emotional world, femininity is formed in a waiting, throbbing desire for the happy ending, the climactic 'I . . . love . . . you', followed, in imagination or on the page, by kiss and penetration. At the same time, sexual desire is endowed with spiritual and moral significance. Every physical detail is simultaneously a mirror of the soul. The desire that romance structures in this way is exclusively heterosexual, patriarchal, sado-masochistic. By sado-masochistic heterosexuality we mean the form of sexual relationship between men and women – the dominant one in our society – in which pleasure is the result of masculine activity and feminine dependence and passivity.

Thus, Cynthia Morrow's unselfconscious beauty, perfect oval face and blue eyes (her whiteness is assumed, not stated) signify her goodness, while Sara Eastwood's 'tinted golden hair' and 'artificially darkened eyes' indicate a woman who is promiscuous in her affections and not to be trusted. This moral distinction between nature and artifice is not, of course, limited to the conventions of romantic fiction; but it is employed in Cartland's writing in a notably loaded and systematic fashion. From the opening page, Robert's dark eyes and masterly gestures signify that this is a proper man, though one whose 'mocking smile' must first be straightened by love.

Clothes and jewellery too reveal the truth. Sara praises Robert's gift of a gaudy dress to Cynthia for her to wear at the ball, instead of an 'old rag' of her own, made in 1939. But Cynthia rejects it, and chooses to wear her own well-cut dress together with a diamond necklace, part of a family collection. This carefully composed exterior betokens the recognition of something less tangible: 'You've got something which is more important than clothes and jewelry' (Cartland 1967, p. 72).

This transference from outer to inner, from physical to spiritual, is basic to romance. The hero must distinguish himself from the other men in the story, rescuing the heroine for a more sacred kind of lust. His kiss provokes a vision of what could be. In all Cartland's novels, the hero commands the heroine to speak, and she must obey before the climactic, consummating kiss can happen:

> 'Say it. Oh, my darling, say the words I am waiting for . . . longed for . . . prayed for.'
>
> Now she must obey him, and falteringly, stumblingly, yet in utter simplicity, she whispered, 'I . . . love . . . you . . . Robert.'
>
> (Cartland 1967, p. 191)

The man is the teacher, the woman his willing pupil. 'Women's sexuality must be awakened,' Cartland has informed us, 'unlike the man's, which arises spontaneously.' The kiss which follows signifies orgasm (Cartland has described sexual consummation as the perfect end of a long, long kiss), and also, for the woman, a *Liebestod*, a transcendental spiritual union like death. The power of this ending is connected to the sense of the ending of the narrative as an experience of loss, as well as to the common connection, in life as in language and art, between sexuality and violence.

> She felt him raise her face to his; they looked into each other's eyes and then, as if their humanity broke beneath the strain, he sought her lips . . .
>
> Closer and closer he held her until a flame seemed to unite them, a flame in which joy and passion, happiness and desire mingled together in an all-consuming love. His kisses became more possessive. She felt as if he drew her very life from between her lips. She forgot the past and the future in an utter surrender of herself . . . she was his . . . his for all time.
>
> (Cartland 1967, p. 192)

In romance, women's desire is a powerful dynamic that structures the plot, even though masochistic, passive, dependent, jealous. Love operates as a code-word for sex, and sexual attraction is conversely a sign that love is present. The major characteristic of this sex-love is that it overpowers man and woman alike. It has the intransitive, irresistible character of a natural force, heat or electricity. It lights fires.

> I also realize that there's a physical excitement between us – a wildfire that ignites whenever we're around each other.
>
> (Simmons 1982, p. 75)

> Life pulsated within her, turning her veins to rivers of molten fire.
>
> (Oldfield 1983, p. 114)

Faced with this impersonal force, all the woman can do is struggle vainly, then 'surrender':

> They fell against each other and, for the first time in their lives, their lips touched gently, reverently at first; then, all restraint washed away, their entwined bodies swayed as if they were locked together in combat.
>
> (Cookson 1974, p. 138)

> As he coaxed her lips apart, she sighed, surrendering to the virile masculinity of his touch and taste.
>
> (Oldfield 1983, p. 72)

> 'We always seem to start out fighting and end up making love.' She curled her arms tight around him. 'That's the way it is sometimes between a man and a woman. It makes the loving that much sweeter, my pet.'
>
> (Simmons 1982, p. 188)

> 'Tell me you'll marry me,' he said.
>
> 'Yes, darling, yes, yes,' she said, with delirious happiness. . . . She cried out in the darkness, 'Please Lorn. Please.'
>
> With a tortured groan, he invaded her, moving slowly, washing her with tide upon tide of desire.
>
> (Oldfield 1983, p. 186)

Male sexuality is an occupying army, female sexuality a country razed by fire, washed by the tide. The pleasures and desires which romances activate and recirculate are the representations of the common form of femininity in our culture.

Juliet Mitchell's account of 'the making of a lady' (Mitchell 1975) gives pride of place to masochism and passivity as the 'marks of womanhood': 'Masochism – pleasure in pain – which is the turning against the self of the wish for the satisfaction of a drive, typifies the feminine predicament' (Mitchell 1975, p. 114). It may be difficult to admit to pleasure of this kind, the pleasure represented, for women, in the sexual codes of romance; but, without such an acknowledgement, only part of the power of romance will be intelligible. A masochistic fantasy such as 'I am being beaten by my father' is 'both a punishment for a forbidden wish and, by repression, a gratification of it' (Mitchell 1975, p. 113). A comparable process occurs in the sexual conventions of romance, which at one and the same time identify women with sexuality (a forbidden pleasure) and constantly defer the sexual consummation of hero and heroine. This deferral takes the form of a struggle – the punishment for a forbidden pleasure: a moral struggle, a spiritual struggle for marriage, a physical-sexual struggle against the overpowering, impersonal force of love. Sexuality is ambivalently gratified and displaced, through the social codes of love-and-marriage, the dominant codes of romance.

*

*Again This Rapture* has served as a basis for an exploration of the major codes and conventions of romantic fiction: its concentration on the private sphere and personal emotion; its marginalization of history and public affairs; its subordination of themes of class and race to those of sex and gender; its spiritualization of sexuality; its sexual masochism; and its repeated promotion of a sexual double standard. Cartland's deployment of these conventions is, of course, her own, and they are differently handled by other writers and at other historical junctures. But their fundamental continuity suggests that they may hold the key to the immense popularity of formulaic romance.

Of course, all those conventions will be found in many different kinds of women's writing; but their presence together in romantic fiction structures a predictable and familiar form of narrative. Like the folk narratives in Benjamin's 'Storyteller' (Benjamin 1973), their repetitions and familiarities serve a didactic end. As popular philosophies, they provide a means of reconciling disparate views and experiences of the world.

Romance conventions are based on a recognition and knowledge of fear and conflict between women and men. Indeed, it is their close, iterative connection with powerful forms of sexual division and subordination that gives them their force. The value they accord to the personal and private sphere allows them to suggest ways of making sense of the world to women whose identity is still shaped by the 'destiny' of housework and childrearing, and who are largely excluded still from full-time work, trade-unionism, politics, the making of 'history'. Of course, the domestic oppression of working-class women is altogether a different process from that of 'Society women', the subjects of a good deal of romance. But there is a common structure of experience. 'Englishness' operates similarly as a common theme, in a form recognizable to all (white) women, placing families – rather than class wealth or enterprise – at the heart of the nation.

But the most important element of all is the resolution of the fictional conflicts and dilemmas, the individual-but-universal happy ending. Rituals of passage from girlhood to womanhood are marked by a process in which separate individuals achieve social recognition and subjectivity as wives and mothers – a process which reinforces the general subordination of women. This movement from individuated to collective identity is reversed in romance. Far from turning 'Cynthia' and 'Robert' into 'Mr and Mrs Shelford', the relationship between hero and heroine is represented as a process of individualization. Each discovers the other's uniqueness. Each singles the other out from the generality of men and women. The love-match that closes the narrative sets the couple apart, while at the same time offering the prospect of a *personal* world of love to every woman. The impossible romantic dream and the social reality of marriage are miraculously reconciled.

The novels also offer a resolution of conflicts organic to modern heterosexual monogamy, of which the most fundamental is the double standard: women must come to their husbands as virgins, while men may, indeed should, be sexually adventurous and experienced in order to 'awaken' the sexuality of their virgin brides. Anyone who doubts whether this code –

and its corollary, the division of all women into virgins and whores – still operates should contemplate the force, in any group of teenage girls, of phrases like 'old slag', 'scrubber' and 'old dog'. In addition to their articulation of this sexual asymmetry, romantic fictions can be conceived as part of a wider battle against 'permissiveness'. Daniel George of the Romantic Novelists Association has defined romances as 'novels which deal with love rather than sex, with courage rather than cowardice, with clean living rather than crime, with questions of right conduct rather than social problems' (Anderson 1974, p. 273). Of course, the defence of virginity will make practical sense for women so long as the double standard continues to operate and the marriage-market system remains the basis of women's material security, the dominant institution for the bearing and rearing of children. Romance recognizes the double standard but redeems its injustices by making the rake-hero vulnerable to love. The virgin-heroine has power: she can reform the rake, and bind him to herself in loving monogamous fidelity.

The spiritualization of sexual desire – like its complementary association with demonic powers – also has a rational basis in a society in which heterosexual 'love' commonly takes the form of disappointed pleasure and even, at worst, brutality. The magic kiss may remind women of a premarital sexuality, of sex as pleasure rather than duty – even though a pleasure contingent on dependence and passivity. Compelled in actuality to service the needs of others, women may find in romance a recognition, quite centrally represented, of their own desires and needs.

Observing the extent to which reality appears turned upside-down in the conventions of romantic fiction, we can register the presence of a powerful ideology which speaks to and resolves in imaginary form many of the most significant and fundamental aspects of women's subordination. That romance comforts women, affirms their value, offers to resolve in imagination conflicts that remain unresolved in reality, while at the same time reconciling them to a subordinate place in that reality, is not a matter for regret or for accusations of false consciousness. Women are not as simply suggestible and credulous as some Marxist and earlier feminist analysis has supposed, and are quite capable of recognizing a fairy-story when they see one. But to respond – even in ironic, ambivalent or self-mocking fashion – to the prince on his white charger, the dark handsome hero with his strong fingers and granite jawline, is to acknowledge implicitly that all is far from well in reality. Romance works with the basic conflict in women's lives. That is what makes it a popular form, and allows the same stories to be told over and over again. Fundamental changes in the genre are likely only when the contradictions that shape women's lives are altered or resolved.

# 6
# Remembering: feminism and the writing of women

> Do not forget:
> The overwhelmingness of the dominant.
> The daily saturation.
> Isolations.
> The knife of the perfectionist attitude.
> The insoluble.
> Economic imperatives.
>
> How much it takes to become a writer. Bent (far more common than we assume), circumstances, time, development of craft – but beyond that: how much conviction as to the importance of what one has to say, one's right to say it. And the will, the measureless store of belief in oneself to be able to come to, cleave to, find the form for one's own life comprehension. Difficult for any male not born into a class that breeds such confidence. Almost impossible for a girl, a woman.
>
> (Olsen 1980, p. 256)

This chapter explores the constraints on and the struggles around writing which have been opened up by the contemporary women's liberation movement. One of the features of this political movement has been its refusal to leave any area of knowledge or experience untouched. Thus feminists have questioned literature and literary values, have established alternatives and have challenged the institutions of literary production and education. This chapter charts that challenge and explores some of the continuing conflicts and tensions.

It is divided into two sections, on criticism and on writing, indicating a separation and a tension that still exist between the two activities. The section on criticism considers four strands of feminist criticism that have been developed in the last fifteen years, and looks at their relationship with work being done in schools, in further and higher education and in adult education. In the section on writing, the focus is on fiction and imaginative writing and the emergence of a feminist culture. This necessarily involves ignoring much women's writing, that which does not directly engage with feminism.

The chapter does not attempt to argue a position, except that which arises from its fundamental premiss that women's writing differs from men's, and that there is political point in asserting and examining that difference. It tries, rather, to set out in some detail the issues that still face feminists engaged with literature, criticism and writing and does not discuss the writing itself.

## Feminism and literary criticism

Prior to questions of feminist criticism is the whole relation we have or don't have to literary criticism generally. Girls are commonly held to be 'good' at English, of all the subjects that women go on to study, English is the most popular, women in teaching are well represented in English and there are women writers firmly established at the heart of the national literature. Yet there are few women professors of English, and the few critics of recognized authority who are women do not derive their authority from what they say either about women or as women. The power of utterance rests with men. Women, as students of literature, are apprenticed to a system which is, despite its reverence or perplexity in the face of a Jane Austen or an Emily Brontë, fundamentally and normatively masculine. Feminist criticism is, at its simplest, a response to this state of affairs.

From the beginning of their long history as writers, women appear to have been conscious that their writing would be judged by a different set of criteria from those used to judge men's writing.

I am obnoxious to each carping tongue
Who says, my hand a needle better fits
A poet's pen all scorn, I should thus wrong
For such despite they cast in female wits
If what I do prove well it won't advance
They'll say it's stolen or else it was by chance.
(Anne Bradstreet, in Bernikow 1979, p. 188)

Is it true, then, to say that feminist consciousness can pre-date by centuries the existence of a political movement that claims it as feminist? It is dangerous to read back into any sign or symptom of female resistance a feminist consciousness. Equally, the cultivation of a simply antiquarian interest in women of the past has its pitfalls. Looking back at women's history, it is important to guard against seeing all women in our own contemporary feminist images, but important too to recognize that women's lives and writings have been shaped by their particular relationship to social life.

By feminist criticism we mean a method of literary analysis that is formed and informed by the politics of feminism – taking the politics of feminism to include all the conflicting, sometimes contradictory strands which currently identify themselves with the women's liberation movement. From such a baseline definition it is possible to stand back and view the recent developments in feminist criticism, with its increasing specialization, particularly in relation to language, as well as its divergences in aim and intention. These differences are the product of different political analyses. It is possible to grasp the recent development of feminist criticism through the history of its organizing concepts, from recovery to revaluation to representation. The object of analysis in feminist criticism changes with the implicit theoretical assumptions employed. At first, women's writing, as the object of criticism, was largely taken for granted. It was simply 'there', to be recovered and revalued.

The absence of women's writing from the canon was seen as an indication of silencing, of the discrimination suffered by women writers. More recently, a situation has developed in which what is meant by 'women's writing' can no longer be taken for granted, and neither 'women' nor 'writing' can be said to constitute a self-evident entity. Analysis is now concerned less with the counting and typifying of women and their experiences, seen as something unproblematic and unified which we recognize from our own unproblematic experience as women. It is concerned rather with the construction and representation of gendered subjectivities, not only in language and fiction but in material life.

This situation has come about in part as a consequence of theoretical developments. The initial impetus came from a Marxist structuralism which had broken with previous forms of social and literary analysis. It attached a prime importance to ideology, and refused simply to acquiesce in a humanist Marxism which was seen as all too similar to the prevailing liberal humanism. It was a profoundly ideological criticism, aiming fundamentally to re-create our relationship as readers to texts and their literariness. In the context of feminism and feminist criticism, this tradition has been developed through an understanding of women's subordination that begins by questioning the unity of the category 'women'. It refuses the simple celebratory implications of that unity which were characteristic of the earliest phases of the current women's liberation movement, with its use of 'sisterhood' as an organizing concept of political action.

Theories that seek to deconstruct what we presently know as women, femininity and the female (as also men and masculinity), and to reconstruct that knowledge through a more thoroughgoing account of our psychic formation as gendered social subjects and our entry into language, have developed considerably over the past five years. The problematizing of 'women' has also had its political consequences, since the 'women' of the women's liberation movement of the seventies were overwhelmingly white, middle-class and heterosexual. In recent years it has become necessary to qualify and expand that definition of 'women' to include women who are working-class, black, of colour, Irish, lesbian. These fracture-lines have run through the whole range of feminist activities, stimulating the production, often as a high priority, of a fiction that seems more adequately to represent those different lives and imaginations. *Outwrite*, for example, is written for a reader who is assumed not to be white British, middle-class and heterosexual. Onlywomen's Press is committed to the development of a specifically lesbian culture. *Spare Rib*, for many years now an outlet for non-professional writing by feminists, has recently asked its white contributors temporarily to cease submitting fiction and poetry.

Within this development there has often been a complementary struggle over language. There has been considerable work recently on the patriarchal nature of language; and in a less theoretical form this has always been a feature of the women's liberation movement. But as yet there has been little discussion of women's relation to language as mediated and determined by their particular class position or their race.

*

We can see, broadly, four strands within feminist criticism. The first follows from Kate Millett's and Mary Ellman's readings of male texts, in that it is concerned with the systematic appearance of ideas and values in literary texts. But whereas Millett and Ellman focused on sexist and patriarchal attitudes in men's writing, some later critics, such as Carolyn Heilbrun, have taken women's writing as their focus and have looked in it for evidence of feminism or androgyny.

The founding texts of modern feminist criticism, *Talking about Women* by Mary Ellman (1968) and *Sexual Politics* by Kate Millett (1972), are marked by their focus on men. Ellman looks to man the critic, Millett to man the novelist. For both, the central concern is women – but women as perceived and represented by men. Between them they provided women involved with literature, as teachers or students, with arguments to counter the sexism in literary criticism. Feminist criticism largely consisted at this stage of different readings of canonical texts, and the principal concern was to break away from the assumption that everyone, women included, must read all texts as if they were written solely for men's pleasure. It became possible for women to consider their femininity as it bore on their reading of male criticism of women's writing, and also to take account of the effects that femininity might be construed to have had on the writing itself. During the early seventies the objects of feminist criticism became increasingly and interestingly diverse, ranging from contemporary male writing to older women's writing, and moving inside and outside the literary canon.

The second strand involves the use of works of fiction to

illustrate social and historical aspects of women's lives. Fiction is used, in this tradition, as a means of introducing, examining and learning about the history of women, and of providing experiential access to past women's lives. Vineta Colby (*Yesterday's Woman* (1974)) and Françoise Basch (*Relative Creatures* (1974)) are examples of critics who have worked in this way.

Of the four strands, this is the one that has been most extensively developed in Britain. *A Very Great Profession* (1983), by Nicola Beauman, is a recent example; but the real impact of this approach has been in teaching rather than in published criticism. British feminist critical projects are far more likely to have a 'literature and society' component than their North American or European counterparts. Feminist criticism in this country has developed in a critical relationship with socialism and Marxist criticism. The form of the critique has been to accept certain tenets of Marxist criticism, including the relating of literature to its social conditions of existence, but to redress the absence from it of women and of any serious consideration of the personal, the domestic and the sexual.

The third strand sees women writers as a group in their own right, rather than relating them, however critically, to a tradition of male writing. Patricia Meyer Spacks in *The Female Imagination* (1976) argues that women are essentially and necessarily different from men, and that this difference is represented in their fiction. Elaine Showalter in *A Literature of their Own* (1978) argues against this essential femaleness, but is concerned nevertheless to show how the subordination of women throughout history has had the effect of constituting women writers (and readers) in a 'subcultural' group apart from, and in opposition to, the dominant male culture.

The three strands discussed so far all coexist relatively peaceably, sharing as they do a clear commitment to literary criticism as a humanist practice. But some recent developments in cultural analysis, while extending to the 'literary', do not confine themselves to it. What is sometimes known as 'deconstructive' criticism has developed as a cultural rather than an exclusively literary form of analysis, drawing on a range of political, psychoanalytical, historical and cultural theories. It sets itself against realism, both as a mode of writing and as a theory of the artistic 'reflection' or 'expression' of a 'real' world, arguing instead that the meaning of a text is diverse, multiple, unstable and always *produced*, by author and reader. This fourth strand currently occupies a difficult and often contradictory place within thinking about women's writing, and indeed within feminist politics more generally.

The energetic dismantling of what is obvious, natural and taken for granted, in writing, criticism and everyday life, has a great deal in common with the way in which feminism as a politics disrupts all that is obvious, natural and taken for granted about women's position and existence. As a critical project, its mistrust of that which confirms and reassures is powerful. Feminism's relation to women's subordination has been strongly driven by the idea and the experience of breaking silences, articulating and expressing things previously undervalued or suppressed. There is a very powerful tradition of 'expression' within the women's liberation movement, which finds what seems to many of its readers and writers a natural home in creative and fictional work.

Deconstructive criticism is not necessarily incompatible with this. In fact it can assist the process in identifying exclusions and helping to clarify the political implications of silences and their breaking. In practice, however, the relationship has so far been a negative one, concentrating on the critique of feminist practices such as consciousness raising (speaking bitterness), and dismissive of feminist fiction which gives primacy to representing the experience of personal change. This strand of feminist criticism is at its most useful in dismantling concepts of literature and literary value, and in providing ways of reading the canon 'against the grain'.

All four strands of feminist work have raised new and important questions which the literary-critical establishment still studiously ignores. But each, in its very different way, leaves a sense of inadequacy. Millett's focus is still on men's writing. Were there no women? The social historian's approach sees no difference between a literary text and a minute book, as historical evidence. The 'subculture' tradition continues to operate within the limits of the canon, and its sense of a unified women's culture has to be questioned. The deconstructionists sometimes seem to reduce the world to a set of discourses operating independently of historical agency.

In general, over and above the particular problems in each of these strands, they have in common a lack of engagement with contemporary writing, and a disabling distance from the practical circumstances and struggles which determine access to creativity. They lack too a sense of the wider contexts in which women read and talk about their reading, particularly those outside and independent of any formal academic structure.

*

Academic literary criticism has a complex relationship with contemporary writing, mediating the formation of literary intellectuals and implicitly informing the practices of publishing and reviewing, while in its own practice ignoring or marginalizing current and recent fiction. The distance between 'literature' and actual contemporary writing is well policed in schools and universities. In schools, in particular, modern fiction is generally a means of cultivating an interest in reading, useful for its 'relevance' but never able to supplant literature and literary value. One of the most exciting possibilities that feminist criticism has opened up is a concern, both literary and political, with contemporary writing. In the furore that followed the publication of Millett's *Sexual Politics*, feminists initiated a major literary debate centred on women. This was important and exciting, but it should have been extended so that feminists could really claim contemporary writing as a proper object of study and work, and so that feminist criticism could speak to contemporary readers about contemporary writing as well as about past traditions.

A good deal of feminist criticism has been organized around the concept of *recovery*: the formalizing of a tradition of women's writing out of the work of 'lost' authors, past and present. This work has its value; but it is not enough simply to catalogue women's writing or to construct unitary continuities in the name of a tradition. We should consider the relation between past and present in the light of the needs given by our current political struggles for women's liberation. We need to attend to the relationship between the continuities and discontinuities in the form and experience of oppression and subordination, especially as determined by race and class. Having grasped that relationship, we must see how it determines both access to writing and publication and the narrative and representational spaces within which women writers work.

Equally, the combative engagement with male writing which Millett began has never been fully taken up. It remains important to examine the ways in which sexism informs and deforms the writing of men; and Mailer, Miller and Lawrence are not the only men ever to have written. What blunted these radical edges of feminist criticism is intimately tied up with the contradictory position it occupies: one foot 'out there' in the women's liberation movement, one foot 'in here' in the academy. And the academy, with its power to dispense money, degrees, jobs, status and prestige, invariably tips the balance in its own direction.

This raises one of the key questions for feminist criticism: should it bring the concerns of women to an already constituted body of intellectual work – literature and literary criticism? Or should it aim totally to transform criticism as we know it, to such an extent that we could no longer speak of literature and literary criticism at all?

The question is a difficult one. We might say that the real emphasis, in the unstable pairing of feminism with criticism, lies with feminism: that the real focus and generation of feminist criticism lies within the women's liberation movement and with feminists who find in writing and reading a medium to express and explore the conflict and pleasure of redefining their place in society. We could argue that feminist criticism is or should be about the needs of feminists working with or responding to the medium of language and fiction: that it is about how, as women and feminists, we do and might read, how we do or might write. Or we could say that the emphasis falls on criticism: that we accept and work on and within the techniques and methods of literary criticism or cultural analysis, but that we bring to them a concern with women's experience which we particularize in relation to writing, and that we introduce, as students and teachers, the non-competitive, non-hierarchical modes of working which feminism encourages. Or we could refuse this way of drawing boundaries and setting up oppositions and say: yes, it is all of this, and a bit more besides.

*

The tensions and contradictions of being in two places, inside and outside education, are central to feminist criticism. For example, to consider in detail the processes of exclusion and devaluation which have rendered much women's writing marginal to 'real' literature, and the anomaly whereby even the 'great' women writers, such as Virginia Woolf, George Eliot, Sylvia Plath and Doris Lessing, come to be considered great without any reference to the fact of womanhood, can lead on to other questions. It can disturb notions of inherent literary value, give the lie to criticism's authority of response, and dispute the inevitability of literary canons. It can pose very sharply the distance between what exists, in our day-to-day experience of it, as valuable and valued writing, and what is consecrated, in the education system, as the national literature. In this way feminist criticism can be compared with other forms of critical work, such as black studies, Marxist criticism and movements to develop working-class writing, which oppose the dominant order. Each makes use of writing, and each imposes its own priorities. What they share, at their best, is the desire to rekindle and foster a creativity dulled and devalued by subordination. The potential of feminist criticism in this direction was, by implication, noted by Kate Millett:

> Literary criticism is not restricted to a dutiful round of adulation, but is capable of seizing upon the larger insights which literature affords into the life it describes, or interprets, or even distorts. . . . I have operated on the premise that there is room for a criticism which takes into account the larger cultural context in which literature is conceived and produced.
>
> (Millett 1972, p. xii)

This suggests a redefinition of the traditional boundaries of intellectual disciplines. The interdisciplinary pull in feminist research has been strong because the political baseline of feminist work in any intellectual field – women's subordination and its effects – can never be explained within the terms of the pre-constituted intellectual disciplines alone. Frequently the move into interdisciplinary work prompts a highly political reassessment of the organization, uses and value of academic work itself. This challenge to an education system which in the process of educating confirms, perpetuates and reproduces division, inequality and misrepresentation constitutes the radical edge of feminist criticism.

However, this can be and has been blunted. Evolving as it did within the institutions of higher education, feminist criticism has been caught between the contradictory demands of the political and academic spheres. At one level there have been the demands of scholarship and tradition which say: 'Before you can question me you must prove your case.' This has brought into existence much valuable work – Showalter's *A Literature of Their Own* being a case in point. We would have a series of disagreements and arguments with that book. It does not give a very satisfactory account of twentieth-century women's writing. There are things to be said about social class which remain unsaid. The desire to hold on to the distinction between 'great' and 'lesser' writers and writings – however redrawn – can be infuriating. The notion of a 'subculture' of women writers (Showalter 1978, pp. 11–15) is insufficiently complex to account for women's relation to the literary mode of production. And yet . . . at the very least, the book's existence has clarified for a great many feminists a whole set of issues arising out of their own reading and research. And, perhaps more important, it has provided substantive ammunition for arguments against the orthodox accounts of women's literary capacity and achievement.

The proving of feminism's case against and to the dominant literary practice – through the rediscovery of traditions of women's writing, the rereading and revaluation of women's writing and the combating of critical theory – has set in motion processes which become all the time more dependent on the internal movements of that which they oppose. Feminist criticism of this kind, valuable as one part of the struggle, runs the risk of ceasing to speak to those women outside or on the fringes of institutional higher education in whose name it often claims to speak. This is not to say that theories or intellectuals are unnecessary, or to discount and ignore what is happening in feminist criticism in higher education – both the positive achievements of that kind of work and the struggles through which it continues to be possible at all. What is necessary is to stop taking higher education for granted as the beginning and end in thinking about reading and writing as they relate to feminist politics. It is time we tried to think about it both 'outside' *and* 'in and against' higher education.

*

We want now to sketch out some practical suggestions about how feminists might approach literature, or rather English, in different educational contexts. One problem, in everything we say, concerns the role of the teacher. Feminist education ought to be about self-determination. It should call into question and substantially alter the relations of power in the teaching–learning situation, and actively question the values, meaning and relevance of lessons. In practice, though, the situation remains a contradictory one. The teacher will still be *telling*: offering her students, from a position of institutional advantage, an avowedly non-hierarchical, egalitarian way of learning, and also, probably, assessing both it and them; and the structural positions of 'teacher', 'pupil' and 'student' reinforce this, as does the hostility that feminism arouses in fellow teachers and many students. There is also a disagreement within feminism itself about whether it is something for women only, or whether it links up with a more general sexual politics that concerns both women and men.

The general feminist principle of non-hierarchical and collective modes of work, together with the absence of a feminist critical orthodoxy, means that theoretically students can be as active and capable as their teachers in the process of producing knowledge. In practice, this is rarely the case. Certain institutional requirements, notably exams, perpetuate the difference between students and teachers. Practically, too, through experience and specialization, teachers usually have more extensive and systematic knowledge than their students. There are material relations within which teachers and students interact with one another: however much feminists may wish to eradicate or minimize these relations of difference, and the power and powerlessness involved in them, they remain beyond the reach of change through individual intent or goodwill.

Schools, where power relations are strongest, are the least likely places for students and teachers to be able to work together collectively. Talking to some women teachers, it seems that the identification and combating of sexism in teaching methods and materials is the key struggle they are engaged in. Many find that feminist criticism, with its inclination towards higher education and postgraduate research, and its sense that the struggle against sexism is a stage on the way to more complex work on representation and signification, does not connect with their needs and interests. A second important factor for feminist teachers is that, unlike feminists engaged in teaching women's studies options in higher education, they will be teaching compulsorily to a fairly equal ratio of girls and boys. This is true for non-feminist option teaching in higher education too, but the plight of the feminist schoolteacher is exacerbated by the fact that there is little space anywhere in her work for the relatively pleasant and inspiring teaching of feminist options. Related to this is the lack of control teachers in general have over what they can teach and how they can organize that teaching – by setting up girls' groups, for example – hemmed in as they are by public-examination syllabuses, by cuts and by a lack of non-regulation textbooks.

The problems that women face here are shared by men too, but they do have a specific dimension concerned with issues of gender, as they do with issues of race and class. The feminist project in these circumstances is to bring to attention the representation of, and determination by, gender in reading and writing.

The first problem is the likely response of hostility, boredom or indifference. Some of this will stem from antagonism to 'women's issues', but it has as much to do, probably, with a disengagement from reading and a general disaffection with school. The second problem concerns the method of working itself: how to set about introducing into classroom discussion books that present difficulties to a feminist reader, whether because of their subject-matter, lack of previous feminist research, or the practice of treating set books in isolation from each other. For example, *A Kind of Loving* by Stan Barstow, *Catcher in the Rye* by J. D. Salinger and *Kes* (originally called *Kestrel for a Knave*) by Barry Hines are novels that frequently appear on GCE and CSE syllabuses, probably because all three deal with adolescents or young adults and their experience of school, work, families and sexuality, and so are assumed to be appropriate and interesting to 15- and 16-year-olds.

If we take *A Kind of Loving*, we can envisage not only the problems this sort of book might present but also some ways of dealing with them. Given the kind of representation of women found in the book, how is it to be read and responded to by girls and by boys? How is a critical relation to the ideas represented by the book to be encouraged? One reading strategy likely to be employed by girls is to identify with the male protagonist. The hero of *A Kind of Loving*, Vic Brown, is dissatisfied with his life, his family and, later, his wife. The process of realizing that his dissatisfaction is so pervasive is represented through his growing estrangement from and distaste for all manifestations of femininity, especially female sexuality. His pursuit of sexual experiences with women becomes the symbol of his sense of failure: he feels empty, let down, cheated by it. But his sexuality is also the root cause of that dissatisfaction. Vic is led astray by sex, 'caught out' by it. Given this, and the stock repertoire of female characters in the book – fussing, heart-of-gold mum, aspiring, snobbish mother-in-law, reliable, only-one-who-understands sister, clinging, naïve girlfriend – in what ways can girl students be encouraged to read and study the text, and to enjoy doing so? And to what degree can feminist concerns, which are inevitably woman-centred, be usefully and comprehensively brought to bear on a text which is almost exclusively structured around masculinity?

There *are* ways of discussing a book like this which draw on feminist ideas. For instance, though the political emphasis of feminist criticism has generally been on women (and men) writing about women rather than on men writing about men, it is as possible to talk about gender in terms of masculinity as it is of femininity. It would also be possible to investigate the ways in which representations of women in the text correspond to representations elsewhere in the period and to a social history of women in the fifties. This might be particularly fruitful, given the class relations presented in the book.

Similarly, it would be possible to talk about the differences between courtship and marriage then and now, and to put into question existing patterns of sexual behaviour by demonstrating the degree to which 'natural' expectations are in fact cultural and socially determined. For example, in this novel and in the trilogy of which it is the first volume, pregnancy is, in formal terms, a key structuring device, as well as a central moral concept or touchstone. This is likely to look very different at a time when contraception is readily available and sexual activity increasingly open.

Finally, the discussion could be broadened so that the novel is situated in its context: the 'rediscovery' of class in the later fifties and the investigation of working-class culture through sociological and literary forms. Within this discussion it would be possible to question the way in which women, by not being portrayed with the same sympathy, variety and depth as men, are marginalized or ignored by this discourse, and to ask why, out of quite an extensive movement in post-war writing, there is only one writer, Shelagh Delaney, who treats the experience of working-class women in sympathetic detail.

*

To feminists outside higher education, those within it, students and teachers, are often seen as having the soft option, and are criticized for their preoccupation with theory, which is thought to be an irrelevant indulgence rather than a practical contribution to politics. 'Academic' is frequently a term of abuse in the women's liberation movement, as it is in the labour movement. But this view is at variance with what actually constitutes feminist study and the practical and political issues that inform it. At the same time, it is undeniable that there are differences of priority, emphasis and language, and that the divisions of race and class within the women's liberation movement are thrown into sharp relief by the question of who is involved in higher education.

In polytechnics and universities, there is more potential than in schools for breaking down divisions between teachers and taught in feminist work, though in the college sector of further education the restrictions are almost as great. In polytechnic courses literature often appears as part of a broadly based interdisciplinary programme, and work on women's writing is undertaken in relation either to other cultural forms such as film and television or to other areas of study such as history and sociology. Some courses do, however, maintain more rigid subject-divisions, approximating more closely to university English courses where historical and sociological modes of analysis are subordinated in the official syllabus and teaching programme. In these circumstances the problem facing the feminist, both student and teacher, is how far a feminist or women's writing option will be ghettoized, given its timetable slot between 2 and 5 on a Friday afternoon, and how far it will act as a power-base from which to intervene in and gradually transform other areas of the degree course. This problem presents itself in different ways to students and to teachers.

In theory the student is free to argue her feminist approach throughout the curriculum. In practice this freedom is sharply curtailed. Feminist criticism and a feminist approach to writing aren't just about finding a 'feminist interpretation' of any pre-given text, though feminist arguments will often be text-centred. This is partly because feminist criticism, in many of its variants, is a text-centred activity; but it is partly, too, because the terms of debate are predetermined. You may want to argue about 'where the women writers in the eighteenth century are', but like as not you'll keep being pulled back to discussions of particular texts and the ways in which they address or comment upon gender. Feminist criticism is about wider issues than selecting texts: ideally, it is about the whole organization and rationale of courses of study.

Let us suppose that a feminist student is taking an eighteenth-century 'Augustan literature' course organized as follows: introductory lectures, with little follow-up in tutorial or essay work, on the history of ideas and the literary history of the period; lectures on 'major authors' – all male; tutorials and essays which invite the student to follow up the itemization of the period broadly suggested by the lectures. This doesn't actually prevent a continual meshing of the particular with the general, but it certainly doesn't encourage it. How does a student with feminist principles but without extensive knowledge of the period respond to this situation? Knowing that feminist ideas, women's writing and women's special gendered relation to the organization of literary production will not have been important (to put it mildly) in the planning and preparation of the course, and lacking the substantive and detailed knowledge needed to back up the case for something different, she will be reduced to making critiques and asking questions that are easy to dismiss, discountenance or ignore. The absence of feminist ideas in the research and training of her teachers, combined with the amount of feminist research that remains to be done and the vast areas of ignorance we still have as women about the history of our sex, means that she is likely to be confined to moral arguments, rather than the intellectual ones that she requires.

These difficulties would be encountered in virtually every literary period except the mid-nineteenth century. As well as the problem of the lack of knowledge in the form of accessible research, there is also the question of the hostility which such a student is likely to encounter. Unpleasant as that might be, no feminist is likely to lose sleep, though she might lose marks, over the fact that certain middle-aged men, failing to find their gallantry met by feminine charm, took a dislike to her. More serious might be the lack of informed discussion of her work, when comments on it are restricted to variations on the theme 'I fail to see the relevance of'. We're not suggesting that she would become the victim of blind prejudice; but if she is getting involved in primary research for the purpose of writing term essays, as opposed to the interpretative and evaluative work which they are designed to assess, she is going to be handicapped in comparison with other students quite happy to work within the existing framework and terms of reference of their degree course.

One solution to all this is to establish informal research and discussion groups composed of undergraduates and postgraduates who share an interest in women's writing. These groups can provide both intellectual and moral support. One which was set up at Birmingham University began as a general reading and study group, and then moved on to consider in detail a particular undergraduate course, on seventeenth-century literature. In this way it was possible to explore, debate and learn about feminist criticism in a context that allowed disagreement, doubt and ignorance to be voiced without fear of conceding the whole feminist argument to the hostile or indifferent. Women who felt an identification with feminist criticism, but who were unable or unwilling individually to challenge tutors and aspects of their course, could help to generate and benefit from collective power. The forum shared experiences of that particular institution, and increased knowledge about women's writing and feminist critical theory through a self-motivated and self-disciplined course of study.

The Marxist-Feminist Literature Collective, on the other hand, was not based in any one institution, and began as a study group to read critical theory, later developing its own projects as the basis for papers delivered at conferences, and led eventually to the formation of the 'Women and Writing' workshops and newsletter. Together these acted as a means of developing contact and discussion between women involved and interested in women's writing at a variety of levels. Sometimes tentatively but rarely antagonistically, it held together interest in writing and criticism from students and teachers in schools, adult and higher education, as well as being used by women whose interest in writing and reading was not formally expressed through the education system.

The Feminist English Group at York University have produced a source-book for transforming the university English curriculum.[19] In their introduction they address the way in which feminism questions the category of 'literature', and suggest other methods of organizing courses of study. More pragmatically, they go on to list the myriad sources and references that refute the defence of courses excluding women writers on the grounds that there never in fact were any.

It is important here to remember that higher education does not monopolize the study of women's writing. Study groups and conferences have been organized independently by and for people interested in discussing or finding out about women writers and questions of feminism and literature. Examples of this are the Barlaston Summer Schools in 1980 and 1981, and women's liberation movement conferences and workshops like the one held in Edinburgh in 1983.[20]

For teachers in higher education there are two methods of working. One is to introduce a feminist perspective and argument into any teaching and lecturing. The second is to develop, argue for and teach special courses in aspects of feminist literary theory and women's writing. The problems likely to be encountered are, first, that a teacher may already be overstretched, with a conventional teaching-load that leaves little time or energy to develop new courses using unfamiliar material, or to rethink existing material from a new and difficult perspective. Linked with this is the relative underdevelopment of feminist criticism when set against the solidity of the modes it challenges, and the need to be 101 per cent sure when arguing in staff and course meetings. This is particularly true in polytechnics, where CNAA validation procedures demand massively detailed submissions not just for every degree course but for all subsequent changes to it. Finally, in addition to conflict at the intellectual level over theoretical issues and the selection of texts for study, there is likely to be conflict over teaching methods. Informal seminar-based styles, with high levels of student participation, continuous assessment and forms of group and collective study will be ranged against a lecture-and-tutorial system which individualizes work and is competitively geared towards formal examinations.

If, as is usual, the method is a course option in women's writing, how can one deal with the attendant marginalization? Related to this is the question of professional specialization which determines exchanges between members of staff. An average English department will have its Marxist and, increasingly, its feminist, as well as its textual critic, Leavisite, biographical critic and linguistician, and its James, Dickens, Joyce and Wordsworth 'men'. Occasions such as staff seminars veer between rituals of display and of confrontation, and under these circumstances women need support from elsewhere, not just to moan about how dreadful X or Y is, but as a forum to discuss ideas, admit ignorances and uncertainties, and develop new work in a milieu where their ideas and principles are taken seriously. Also, women in different institutions can learn from each other about designing and teaching courses. A further advantage of networks which cross and link educational institutions is that they enable wider perspectives on individual institutions to develop. It is vital that feminists in schools, in further education, in higher and in adult education should share their individual working experiences with one another. Equally vital, though more likely to fall victim to expediency, is the need to develop an overall sense of feminist culture and a perspective which links it to feminist interventions in literature across the educational system.

Schoolteachers and undergraduate students have, on the whole, little opportunity to engage in feminist research. University and polytechnic teachers are more likely, because of the pressure to publish in order to gain tenure and promotion, to be involved in research, but a considerable amount of feminist research is done by women postgraduate students.

Much feminist criticism today originates – and remains – as research undertaken within higher education. This has its good and its bad sides. It is a site for the clarification of theoretical issues and for the general advancement of knowledge about the subject, filling in absences and providing material of use to students and teachers. On the negative side, there are two quite distinct orders of difficulty. On the one hand, postgraduate research is in general a very isolated and lonely activity. In the past, women's relation to research has been that of a succouring helpmate, servicing a male researcher, with the reward of becoming the wife of a junior lecturer in the future. Women doing postgraduate research themselves generally find there is a lack of people prepared to perform such functions for them.

More seriously, there is the problem of supervision. Feminists are not well represented in English departments, and either supervision goes by default, with women struggling on as best they can, or there is a constant battle between student and supervisor. Sometimes supervision is spread between several people, and much letter-writing and informal talking takes place. Valuable as this is, it can be a strain on both sides.

Another difficulty is whether the individual researcher can link up with the needs of the women's liberation movement, of feminist writers and readers and of other feminists engaged in research – whether, indeed, that responsibility is even recognized. It is the case, too, that, even where such accountability is acknowledged, it is difficult to tap into it. One consequence of this has been the narrowly antiquarian interest of many theses in the most obscure women of the past. The neatly packaged commodities of the literary-critical industry encroach into women's studies in literature and distance research from current political concerns. This tendency is exacerbated by the influence of the academic market, and of publishers constructing feminist lists as much to cash in on one of the few expanding areas in publishing as to advance the development of a political culture.

*

Finally, we can consider an area where many of the institutional restraints – exams, competitive individualism – disappear, only to be replaced by others like weather, fatigue, absence of financial support and lack of status for students and teachers. This is the area of adult education, itself not a unitary field. The Workers' Educational Association, for instance, has passed motions at its annual conference which commit it to promote women's studies, and it supports the only women's studies newsletter in the country. Yet it consistently refuses to employ a women's education worker who might help to realize that commitment in practical terms, and in some districts women have to defend their women's studies courses and their women-only classes against charges that they are discriminatory and/or not properly 'educational'. The WEA does, though, compare favourably with some university extramural departments, which even if they have feminists on their staff are rule- and custom-bound by the imperative to provide adult education of appropriate university standard in appropriate university subjects, which of course do not include women's studies. In some respects adult education, with its relative flexibility of commitment, its freedom from competing and 'qualifying', has been a most productive site for women's studies and feminist education. Women who could not or do not want to go to college full-time can fit in an evening or an afternoon once a week. And women who for various reasons, not always of their own choosing, cannot work full-time find the opportunities for part-time teaching useful. An interest in reading can lead, on these courses, into an interest in women's writing and through that to a political interest and involvement in feminism. Women who would not choose to go to courses on 'women in society' may wish to attend a class on women's writing. This flexible approach to changing educational needs is unique to adult education, even if it is not always fully realized there.

Women's writing, as an area of study, is relatively open in adult education. Most important, perhaps, is the ease with which it can be detached from literature. This is not to say that the very necessary arguments about why women's writing is as valid and as valuable, in literary terms, as any other literature, and why literary value as presently understood doesn't matter, are being ignored there. Rather they are short-circuited, and feminists are free to construct forms of study which start from different premisses. For example, a course offered at Thames Polytechnic, on 'Women's lives and writings from 1900 to 1945', draws on a range of fiction, autobiography and historical documentation to examine the changing experiences of women's lives and the various forms of their representation in an exciting and original way. The other great advantage of adult education's concern with women's studies is that it makes it relatively easy for readers to become writers. Women attending writers' workshops, which are designed to study the women's own writing, quite often find that they want to read and discuss the work of published writers – either 'famous' or from other workshops; and, conversely, those attending classes that are primarily concerned with reading published writers may develop an interest in recording and fictionalizing aspects of their own lives.

*

As this outline has indicated, feminist criticism can exist within different educational sites in a variety of forms. It is a combative criticism. It has developed in opposition to orthodox literary criticism, which has ignored women's consciousness, marginalized their literary productions by assuming masculinity and male experience to be normative, and neglected their experiences and pleasures of reading. More recently, feminist criticism has taken issue with a Marxist criticism that in its challenge to capitalism continues to assent to patriarchy. Against all this, feminist criticism has placed sexual politics on a par with class politics, matching theoretical advances in culture and ideology with their practical extension and development in gender-differentiated terms. The greatest handicap of feminist criticism is that it is constituted 'against' rather than 'for' something. Developing as a critique of existing practices, it has often failed to examine what exactly feminist criticism is for, both in terms of its long-term commitments and of *who* it is for – male critics, female critics, writers or readers?

These considerations refer us to the problem mentioned earlier: whether the emphasis in feminist criticism should fall on 'feminist' or on 'criticism'. It has been, and continues to be, argued that the initial project of feminist criticism must be against literary criticism itself. The argument runs that there is nothing to be gained, for women, from their insertion into preconstituted canons of literature and into critical procedures as ideologically questionable as literary criticism. This argument, which is decidedly persuasive, leads on to a simple question: why does writing matter? But it doesn't effectively clarify the predicament of those feminists for whom, because of the institutional structures in which they find themselves and because of their general commitment to education and the value of research, the struggle must of necessity be fought on the terrain of literary-critical theory and practice. For these women, the fundamental challenge to literary criticism, even if they believed it necessary, could never as yet result in actually overthrowing it, and they are thus isolated from the political movement that should sustain them. Feminism is in real danger of creating its own élites, leaving most women and women's issues as isolated and undervalued as ever.

## Feminism and writing

> Are there no husbands, lovers, brothers, friends to cuddle and console? Are there no stockings to darn, no purse to make, no braces to embroider? My idea of a perfect woman is one who can write but won't.
>
> (Lewes 1850, p. 189)

> The literary novel is a field of art in which only fools would say that women's achievement is less than men's, a field in which there need only be critical reasons for distinguishing men's and women's contribution to it. . . . Only my enemies, it has been said, can make me a Jew or a black, or, so far as the writing of novels goes, a woman.
>
> (Laski 1981, p. 7)

Times change but, as the admen put it, values don't. One constant strand of feminist intervention in the sphere of writing is the challenge to the dominant value-system and the gradual construction of alternative ways of valuing the writing of women. Much of this struggle has been over ideas and meanings, a way of defining the project of feminist critical activity in education. But there have also been, and continue to be, material changes which produce and sustain a feminist cultural alternative. 'Writing' is more than the words on the page, or the physical activity of putting them there. To register socially, to acquire meaning and value, writing must be available, on a larger scale than is possible in hand-to-hand personal circulation. This involves institutions and activities beyond the individual writer: publishers, bookshops, libraries, the Arts Council and its regional arts associations, literary journalism, and the infrastructure of bursaries, grants and prizes.

The terms 'woman' and 'feminist' slide around. At times they seem interchangeable, at times distinct if not actually opposed. This ambiguity characterizes women's writing today. Not all women are feminists, and not all women's writing is feminist writing. The cultural institutions referred to earlier can best be described as elements or potentialities of a feminist culture. The political impulse behind their formation involves an appeal and an openness to all women. But in practice participation in and identification with this culture, by women as opposed to feminists, is restricted.

Raymond Williams, discussing the processes of cultural change, has pointed to the need to distinguish between those changes 'which are really elements of some new phase of the dominant culture . . . and those which are substantially alternative or oppositional to it: emergent in the strict sense, rather than merely novel' (Williams 1977, p. 123). Feminists, well aware of the extent to which capitalism packages and markets versions of womanhood to women, are rightly suspicious of attempts to capitalize on feminism. However, the processes by which radical movements are robbed of their potential can take very subtle forms. Retaining the advantages of capitalist forms and ways of working, through which radical ideas and activities gain a degree of legitimacy and a greater visibility, can be very difficult, and even at best is never wholly within the control of individuals and small cultural institutions. The danger of rejecting any involvement in existing forms is the complete marginalization of the activity. The charge of 'preaching to the converted' is often laid at the door of feminists, as of other oppositional groups. Another way of denigrating radical work is to claim that its successes have been achieved in spite of, and are therefore detachable from, its political genesis and intent. Thus Marghanita Laski, in a review to mark the Virago Press's fifth birthday, correctly identifies its political importance and oppositional intent, and then proceeds to undermine it. Books are books, literary values are literary values, and feminism is a bit of a joke:

> The decision, then, of a publishing house staffed and advised by women to devote itself to the republishing of good novels only if they are of special female interest and/or sensibility must strike the general reader as a sadly not gladly limiting choice. . . . But generally, within and not making allowance for their chosen brief, Virago's choice of novels is admirable. I take this as consoling evidence that, whatever the rationalizations, trained critical sensibilities will tend to reach consensus on quality.
>
> (Laski 1981, p. 7)

'Preaching to the converted' is not a completely valueless activity; but all cultural practice that claims a commitment to and an involvement in change must also work to develop ways of contesting the status quo, of converting the unconverted. The main task for feminists active in literary culture is to present alternatives that are genuinely oppositional.

Compared with ten or even five years ago, feminist literary culture is thriving and expanding. In Britain there are five publishing houses committed to the publication and reprinting of works by and of interest to feminists. There has also been a marked increase in the number of women's imprints and lists within mainstream publishing. Four of the feminist publishers are in London, and one in Edinburgh – a pull towards the metropolis indicative of its continued dominance in intellectual life, a dominance reproduced in the institutions of alternative culture.

Each of these publishers has its own priorities, style and scale of operation. The oldest of them, Virago, was established in 1976 and holds the largest backlist, predominantly reprints in the Virago Classics series. This publishing venture is the one most intimately linked to developments in education. Feminist research, and the teaching of courses on women and literature, are made possible in some cases and easier in all by the ready availability of texts. Virago has earned some criticism from feminists for its 'packaging', for its adherence to the idea that there is a *single* tradition of women's writing hidden in the past and that a simple recovery is possible and desirable, for taking over the term 'classic' and applying it too freely to all or most non-contemporary women's fiction, and for its concentration on past writing at the expense of encouraging and promoting the new. Some of these criticisms are valid; but it must be remembered that Virago, in making women's fiction with a feminist appeal a viable publishing option, has done more than test the market for mainstream publishers or compromise feminists. Bookshops that refuse to carry radical publications do stock certain Virago titles; and in this way those books and the ideas in them become available to a wider public. Books alone will not effect a political mobilization of women, will not convert the unconverted; and it is a mistake to view the bookshop in isolation from the social and cultural relations around it. But the availability of these books in High Street bookshops is one link, and an important one, in the chain.

The other publishing enterprises – the Women's Press (set up in 1978), Onlywomen Press (1976–7), Sheba (1979–80) and Straumullion (1980) – concentrate far more on contemporary fiction and poetry, and the Women's Press list reflects a commitment to the republication of black American and European writing. Of these, only the Women's Press is comparable in scale to Virago. Straumullion is currently publishing one book at a time. Sheba publishes six to eight books a year and initially relied very heavily on pre-publication orders for finance; it has a commitment to the publication of writing for children and young women, with a strong anti-racist component. Onlywomen Press publishes up to four titles a year, in pamphlet as well as book form, and gives priority to the writing of lesbians.

The women's liberation movement has maintained a strong journalistic tradition of women's writing. *Spare Rib*, the monthly magazine of women's liberation, carries fiction and poetry regularly. Once in a while it publishes a translation, like the Russian serial 'A week like any other', or extracts from a new book; but its major role is to publish new work by women who would not style themselves 'writers'. *Spare Rib* has also published important articles about women's writing, and reviews new fiction and poetry by women. The newsletters and papers produced by local women's groups reflect this wider interest in writing by women with book reviews and the publication of writing by readers. Publications of this kind give far more attention to imaginative writing than to criticism or theory, and this may indicate that, for many women active in the WLM, fiction and poetry are a source of knowledge and ideas at least as important as non-fictional or analytic accounts of women's experience and position. Other journals which have appeared over the past few years, catering for more specialized interests, include *Feminist Review*, *Women's Studies International Quarterly*, *Manushi*, *WEA Women's Studies Newsletter*, *Trouble and Strife*. All have devoted some space to the question of women's writing.

There have also been, over the years, a number of newsletters and journals directly concerned with women and writing. The earliest of these, *Women's Liberation Review*, developed out of a workshop on 'Women and literature' at the national Women's Liberation Movement Conference in 1972. Its founding ideas are interesting in that each subsequent publication in the same field has repeated and developed that opening statement.

> Most of us were women writing in the isolation of our own homes who wanted to share our experiences, communicate our ideas.
>
> (*Women's Liberation Review* (1972), p. 3)

> Each piece of writing is like an open letter to all women. The contents were edited and illustrated by women, typed up and laid out by them. The reply we want is for more women to realize they can do the same.
>
> (Northwest Women 1980, Introduction)

> The continued resistance to women writers, combined with the small number of journals in the UK publishing poetry, short stories and essays, results in contemporary women writers involved in these forms finding it difficult to get into print.
>
> (*Writing Women* (1981), p. 1)

The other principle on which *Women's Liberation Review* was founded was the desire to generate writing responsive to the situation, concerns and aspirations of feminist women. That problem – the complete absence of cultural forms which speak to and of a changed situation – has been gradually overcome through the republication of 'lost' works by feminists addressing similar concerns. It has been overcome too by the creation of conditions enabling the production of contemporary writing which bears very clearly the marks of its encounter with feminist ideas and lifestyles. The current feminist writing scene is strong and buoyant enough to allow different emphases to emerge within it. *Spinster*, a quarterly magazine of creative work, gives priority to writing by lesbians. *Writing Women*, a Newcastle-based journal, publishes criticism and creative writing by authors both known and unknown. Publications from groups within the Federation of Worker Writers and Community Publishers give voice to working-class women's experience. Black women writers like Grace Nichols and Valerie Bloom are beginning to break through their double oppression as women and as black people and to gain recognition.

Within the mainstream of literary culture, too, feminism has gained a visibility over the years which is now beginning to register certain effects. First, there has been the willingness of mainstream publishers to publish books which make feminism their starting-point. Frequently the marketing of these books has been sharply at odds with the feminist ideas and intentions of their authors. The kind of promotional publicity given to Lisa Alther's *Kinflicks* by Penguin, and the publicity hype around Marilyn French's *The Women's Room* and *The Bleeding Heart*, are extreme cases of this; though, as the furore about the cover of Susie Orbach's *Fat is a Feminist Issue* shows, protest can sometimes be effective. But for some authors, like Sara Maitland, for example, the opportunity of publishing with a mainstream publisher rather than a smaller feminist one has been chosen because of the possibility of reaching a wider audience in Britain and abroad, and particularly in North America.

Secondly, feminism has begun to enter into the discourse of the major review outlets for contemporary books. Women's writing of any period tends to be perceived in relation to ideas about women's writing – what it is, what it should be, often by implication suggesting what women themselves are or should be. It is rarely considered simply as writing, almost always as writing by women, with even now connotations of inferiority to writing by men – or rather to *writing* pure and simple, since men's writing is never specified in that way.

It appears that the defining mode for the late seventies and early eighties is that of feminism. A defining mode acts to mark the differences between women writers at any given time, but each mode claims to be the appropriate form for women's writing. One index of feminist achievement is that over these years a concern with issues common to writing by feminists – characterizations of women as independent, but as working out relations of dependency and independence in terms of men, marriage and children, together with a degree of formal experimentation – began to appear in the work of contemporary women novelists not identified with the women's liberation movement, and also in reviews of their novels. The transformation of the defining mode of contemporary women's writing to that of feminism is not straightforward. It reflects at times a genuine commitment to feminism as a political movement, if not a cultural one; but it can just as easily testify to a deformation of feminist ideas. The political effectiveness of a cultural form is truncated when that form is detached from its social and political roots and taken up as a source of energy and vitality to bolster moribund cultural traditions. Virginia Woolf wrote:

> Literature is no-one's private ground; literature is common ground. Let us trespass freely and fearlessly and find our own way for ourselves. It is thus that English literature will survive this war and cross the gulf if commoners and outsiders like ourselves make that country our own country, if we teach ourselves how to read and how to write, how to preserve and how to create.
>
> (Woolf 1947, p. 125)

This contains a certain ambiguity. If literature in the abstract is valuable and worth preserving, then the feminist trespass is to the good, and the processes referred to earlier in connection with changes in the defining mode of women's writing are justified. The feminist analysis of culture, however, has involved a more fundamental critique of literature and literary institutions. As we suggested in the discussion of feminist criticism, righting the wrongs of women in literature involves an examination of the very idea of a unitary literature, an established canon of classic texts selected out from writing or fiction in general. In these circumstances, the process of making feminism central to women's writing may be a kind of incorporation. The pull towards a process of containment can be seen most clearly when we consider the proliferation of publishing ventures which have made women's studies into one of the few growth areas in contemporary publishing.

Finally, in considering the situation of the woman writer now, we look at the actual process and practice of writing: not at individual writers, and certainly not at famous or established ones, but at writing workshops with a largely working-class membership. The workshop is a method of organizing which has been taken up and developed by both the women's liberation movement and the worker writer movement, as exemplified in the Federation of Worker Writers and Community Publishers. Both movements share some common elements but are far from identical. Most obviously, questions of class and race have significantly different meanings within the women's liberation movement compared with the worker writer movement. Increasingly it appears that there is a powerful opposition developing here between 'women' and 'feminists'. It is not that the women in these workshops are anti-feminist, but rather that they cannot locate or, if they can, identify with the current organization of the women's liberation movement. In some cases, it is true, they are not looking for the women's movement, having internalized certain of the culture's myths about feminists as extreme, intolerant dogmatists. In the media, the feminist is typically presented as a lesbian; and it is possible that, as some aspects of women's rights and self-determination gain respectability, the feminist project as a whole is discredited through the manipulation of powerful sexual taboos. Women who come to a women writers' workshop may say that they wouldn't have come if it had styled itself 'feminist writers'. Often they don't know exactly what they mean by the difference, but they recognize the distinction and their sense of exclusion.

The writer who most tellingly articulates the different conception of writing generated through feminism is Tillie Olsen.

> We must not speak of women writers in our century . . . without speaking also of the invisible, the as-innately-capable, the born to wrong circumstances – diminished, excluded, foundered, silenced. We who write are survivors, '*only's*'.
>
> (Olsen 1980, p. 39)

That set of ideas and sense of cultural opposition are not just found between the pages of one book, or many. They are found at small writers' workshops started by women up and down the country, where the myth of the struggling individual genius is quashed by the evidence that writers and their writing are the better for working collectively. 'By "better" we mean more honest, more true to our own experiences, more understandable to others' (Cherry *et al.* (eds) 1980, p. 7). They are found in the introductions to collections of writing ranging from the streakily duplicated to the glossy covers which have begun to appear in recent years.

> *Women and Words* has been about finding a new definition for writing, a legitimate place for it in our day-to-day lives.
>
> (Women and Words, 1980, p. 2)

> We hoped we might encourage other women to write, to feel good about writing, to share and publish their poetry too. We don't think of ourselves as being 'special' because we write, and hope you won't either.
>
> (Cherry *et al.* (eds) 1980, p. 8)

This democratization of the cultural practices of writing and publishing, along with a refusal to see politics as something that undermines creativity, reducing it to the status of propaganda, entails its own order of problems. The underlying assumption that writing is a special and an important activity, but that writers themselves are not special, are ordinary everyday people, and that the language they write in does not need to be specially 'literary' either, opens up major areas of debate and contention. One such arises when this assumption is used to create not just an alternative literary culture but an opposition to the existing cultural forms and institutions. Another arises within the literary culture we create and its processes of creation. First, each of us, however far from the dominant literary culture we may have moved or started out from, has been formed in a very direct relation to it. It has its effects, not only on how we write and what we write about, but on how we view our own and other people's writing. For many people the consequence of this is an estrangement from writing itself, an inability to perceive its pleasure, value or relevance. For some, the notion of 'real' writing is almost overwhelming. Their own or their peers' writing always remains somehow amateurish to them, of a different order from 'literature.'

These are fundamental problems, which will determine whether or not a cultural intervention such as establishing a writers' workshop, building up the circulation of a magazine or publishing a book gets off the ground. Once such a project is under way, another set of questions comes into play. These originate in the decision not to separate politics from culture, and have been aptly expressed by one writing collective as 'three timidities. First, and most basic: is my experience important enough to write about? Second: is it important or "right on" in relation to the Women's Movement? Thirdly: is it Art?' (Fell 1978, p. 1). Each of these questions implies a collective situation for the writer. It is her relation to other writers of broadly the same orientation and commitment that sets off the interplay between question and answer. One major advantage of group work and of the writers' workshop model of literary productivity is that it enables a high degree of self-consciousness about writing – its values, achievements and uses – to be used positively. When an individual sits down to write for herself or for some nebulous 'audience' – be it the women's liberation movement or the public 'out there' – such questioning may hamper or prevent writing. In a group context it is capable of being turned into a source of both creative and critical energy in relation to that writing. In this way the workshop can generate a valuable bonding among its members, which often acts as a basis for the exchange of ideas beyond the literary and for the deepening of social relationships based on locality, social group or shared experience.

Those critical of the writers' workshop movement find in this a major justification for their refusal to take it, and its literary products, seriously: it is therapy masquerading as art. In defence we have to return to those fundamental historical and political questions about the place and function of 'art'. So long as it remains the preserve of a few, reified and abstracted from everyday experience, aspirations towards it, towards 'being an artist', will inevitably be considered pretentious, bogus or pathetic. The worker-writer movement generally, and the feminists within and alongside it, are not directed towards gaining acceptance and approval within the present organization of literary production and value. They are motivated by the determination to reclaim the creative resources systematically denied to most people. They are concerned with the task of creating and sustaining the possibility and the imagining of change. Perhaps it is hopeless utopianism to maintain a stake in the imaginative possibility of totally transforming the status quo; but the concrete and practical instances of change to which both the worker writers' and the women writers' workshops can testify remain firmly rooted in the present – a present, too, stamped with its own brand of material deprivation, injustice and misery.

Feminists involved in this process inevitably face a major dilemma about where to direct their energies in the struggle. For some women within the Federation of Worker Writers and Community Publishers, the choice is posed even more sharply in terms of whether to work in mixed groups, coming together on the basis of class or not. Do they work within the limits of a specifically *feminist* culture, producing images and artefacts to reflect, inspire, chivvy and comfort women in the work of being feminists? Or do they direct themselves to the general situation of *women* without, initially, an overt or exclusive focus on *feminist* concerns? At this stage there is room and need for both emphases, provided we can maintain a sense of common purpose and an ability to communicate with one another. Sara Maitland's description of the expectations imposed on feminist novelists and their work is equally relevant in the context of a general cultural strategy for feminism, women and writing:

> We must demand and respond to more novels and better novels, but we cannot demand that one novel must be simultaneously:

> (a) satisfying to our sense of the complexities of our lives,
> (b) a paradigm of orthodox feminism,
> (c) an evangelizing document to convert the unconverted,
> (d) the bearer of a whole new language and symbol structure and world model,
> (e) a good read – witty, inspiring, identifiable-with,
> (f) able to provide us with mythological heroines,
> (g) an exposition of the fullness of women's oppression.
>
> (Maitland 1979, p. 206–7)

We began this chapter by quoting Tillie Olsen on the difficulty of writing, of being a writer. For some women, the existence of writers' workshops and the expansion in the number of outlets for women's writing have begun to ameliorate some of these difficulties. For others, probably the majority, the problems remain as intractable as ever. In *Women's Liberation Review*, one of the first examples of contemporary feminists' involvement with literature, Lee Sanders Comer wrote an article exploring 'how married women are defined as "housewives" whatever their occupation and how their role depends on a denial of self, a forgetting of who they might have been'. It is not directly concerned with the question of creativity, but its final paragraph states in very stark terms the position from which the greater part of our work to stimulate, discover and value the creativity of women must start:

> The gap between the known potential – who you once were and wanted to be – and what your housewife role has turned you into, is enormous and, in most cases, unbridgeable. The hordes of happy housewives that every man testifies to when the role of women is being discussed are simply those women who have successfully forgotten who they might have been. The act of forgetting is their only contribution to the world.
>
> (*Women's Liberation Review* 1972, p. 19)

# 7
# Some women reading

This chapter is a good deal more provisional than the rest of the book: a report of our thinking about readers and reading, rather than a substantive argument or exposition of the issues. We think it worthwhile none the less to share these ideas, and hope that they may stimulate others to go beyond our own very sketchy beginnings.

We became interested in reading and – rather a different matter, so far as most 'theories of reading' are concerned – in *readers* when we realized that our work, for all its anxiety to distance itself from mainstream literary criticism, actually stood, in this respect at least, in a direct line of continuation with it. For, like almost all other literary critics, we were simply *assuming* that we knew what reading was, as an undifferentiated and unproblematic activity, performed by some wholly abstract entity called 'the reader'. So we started by attempting to draw out and analyse these assumptions and to understand their implications. We began with ourselves, with our own practices as readers. If *we* could and did read 'against the grain' of literary criticism's implied or assumed reader – and our whole project assumed that we could – then the notion of a stable, unitary reader, inside or outside the text, was clearly useless, and the way was open for all sorts of other readings. We began to see, too, not only that many readings (in the sense of decodings) are possible of the 'same' text, but that reading itself (as an activity) is very far from uniform. It means quite different things to different people, and to the same people in different circumstances and at different times in their lives, as well as being differentially available, and differently valued, in different sections of society. And this suggested in its turn that the political potential of texts and readings was never a closed matter, and would vary according to circumstance.

Our own reading, we came to think, was of broadly three kinds: reading as *work*, reading for *pleasure*, and reading as part of a process of political education. We then took the same questions to readers whose practice fell quite outside the range of literary criticism, theory or textual analysis – 'ordinary' or 'common' readers. But throughout we never posed the question of reading as an acquired skill, for children or adults; and we now see this complacent assumption of a baseline 'universal literacy' as a myth, and a serious weakness in the work. We would now frame the whole enquiry rather differently, since access to literacy is fundamental to the politics of culture, and the question is not just of different 'kinds' or 'levels' of literacy but of the relation to it of those who cannot or do not write or read at all.

For this project we looked at a number of approaches to reading, and we outline them briefly here in order to contextualize the following account of our own empirical investigations. We looked at theories of reading that draw on psychoanalysis and semiotics. We consulted surveys of reading. And we conducted a number of interviews, in the hope of inaugurating a larger ethnographic study of reading. This project remains uncompleted, and may well stay that way. We report it partly for the important questions that it raises, and partly for the light it throws on some of the other chapters, where an adequately complex and historical understanding of 'the reader' remains implicit, at best.

The enquiry began with questions about women's relations to reading, as a way of highlighting and challenging the 'he' who is, without exception, the implicit subject of dominant literary discourse. But, as it proceeded, the importance of class and of subordinated ethnic cultures in determining the relation of readers to texts, and of the whole network of social relationships within which reading, however 'private', takes place, forced itself to our attention and made it impossible to consider even 'women readers' as an undifferentiated category.

All the women who conducted this study of reading have degrees in English literature. This means that we had been schooled, through GCE literature courses, to give a particular kind of detailed attention to literary texts. By the age of 18 we all had a close knowledge of two Shakespeare plays, a modern poet and a nineteenth-century novel – in most cases the same ones. And we had all been trained to read in a literary-critical way. We were apprentices to the trade of criticism, learning to become the reader that all literary criticism assumes: educated, responsive to the text, attentive, masculine, in command of and fully engaged by the high culture of the Anglo-American élite.

When we asked ourselves 'Why English?' 'Why did we take on that particular apprenticeship?', our attempts to answer immediately revealed the extent to which even this tiny minority of readers falls short of a unified ideal. There are many forces in play which make it far easier for young women to 'opt' for English, including the sexual divisions of the school curriculum and the wider cultural processes of sexual stereotyping; but, even leaving aside these impersonal pressures, the choice to do English was, for us, always ambivalent and full of contradictions. We can remember the horror at 'tearing books apart' – analytical routines that robbed reading of all its pleasure. We remember too the way in which our own pleasure in reading, in 'being a bookworm', was seen as an indulgence by our families, and how O-level literature legitimized that pleasure and, in their eyes, that indulgence: it must be all right to read novels if she can pass an exam in it! How English then became 'work', threatening the pleasure that had drawn us to it in the first place. Some English graduates insist that they will never read a novel again after finishing finals, and in all probability some never do. And yet, work or not, English was still valued less than engineering, medicine, the natural sciences, the subjects the boys had 'chosen', back in the third and fourth years.

Examining our own formation as readers, one of the clearest things to emerge was the paradox whereby reading fiction became a kind of work. This was especially striking for those of us who had gone on to postgraduate research, for which one of us was reading romances, another the work of contemporary women novelists. It became clear that our reading of these texts did not approximate either to our own readings of the same books at other times and in other contexts or to the reading of the women who constituted the greater part of their readership. Mapping out these differences, we began to look too for similarities and points of contact, ways of bringing these different kinds of reading closer together again.

At this stage the focus was primarily on gender, though the question of class determination was inescapable too, given the differences between our own social backgrounds. Class had certainly influenced both our access and our attitudes to reading-matter, some of us being encouraged to read books from an early age, while others applied the word to weekly magazines. But as women we found that we shared many common experiences of reading – using it, for example, to negotiate otherwise difficult or vulnerable situations. By ourselves in pubs, eating out or travelling on trains, we used books to set limits around ourselves, in much the same way in which, we later discovered, the women we interviewed used them.

As well as these convergences in the conditions and tactics of reading, we found similarities in our histories of political reading, of books that had contributed to our political awareness. For some of us a commitment to the women's liberation movement had been closely connected with the importance of reading. Books like Simone de Beauvoir's *The Second Sex* and Juliet Mitchell's *Women's Estate* had had a major influence in the formation of a feminist consciousness; and groups of women meeting formally and informally had exchanged titles and authors, swapped books and discussed fictional situations and characters in terms of what they had to say about our relation to each other, to men, to the world. As for sexuality, and lesbianism in particular, books like *Ruby Fruit Jungle* were a source of knowledge and discussion that simply wasn't available anywhere else. In this kind of reading, pleasure and work converged, for the pleasure lay in part in the work of making sense of our experience in relation to a consciousness of femaleness and femininity. Fictional situations provided one set of indicators against which to think about actual experience, as well as a source of knowledge about the lives of women in situations different from but also recognizably like our own, reinforcing that anger and solidarity about women's position from which feminism developed.

In defining our own histories of reading in terms of work, pleasure and politics, we tried to understand those categories themselves as socially produced, as ideological constructions determining what we read, how we read and to what effect. At the same time, though, we tried to retain a sense that all reading, even the most casual or inconsequential, involves a kind of *work*, a labour of recognition and interpretation, though the *experience* of reading is structured in such a way that the complex and layered work of decoding is hidden under the seeming transparency of meaning. But the question of the 'common reader', the question – never asked by literary critics – of what ordinary, non-professional readers do with poems and novels and stories, continued to nag at our curiosity, and the latter part of this chapter records our early, brief attempts to find out.

As well-trained academics the first place where we looked for answers to our questions about reading was in books by other academics. Peter Mann's surveys of reading habits, particularly his survey, for the publisher, of the readers of Mills and Boon romances, proved a useful starting-point. True, his researches tell us little about the 'inside' of reading, the sense readers make of fiction and the variety of meanings and values they attach to it. But at least his surveys are rooted in social observation, in a way literary criticism almost never is. This kind of market research and sociography of readers can provide a detailed map of the readership of a particular genre. It is thus well suited to studies of popular literature, and has the virtue of taking seriously a kind of fiction which doesn't often find its way into English departments.

A second direction lay in psychoanalytic studies of reading. Literary theorists as well as psychologists have argued that the ways in which literature communicates meaning and pleasure can best be understood by the application of psychoanalytic categories. In one version, the text itself is 'psychoanalysed' on the analogy of a dream narrative or set of neurotic symptoms, for the silences, absences and associational chains that will disclose its 'real' meaning. This procedure tells us nothing, of course, about any actual readers (except, in undisclosed ways, about the critic performing the analysis). Norman Holland's

*Five Readers Reading* suggests a more useful psychoanalytic approach, since it shifts attention from texts to readers' decodings of them. Holland analyses not texts but each of his five readers' retelling of texts. This study has the advantage of recognizing the complexity of the intellectual and psychic processes involved in even the simplest act of reading, and of returning the work involved to concrete human agents. Texts, after all, can do nothing unless they are read by someone. Even so, many difficulties remain. Is it possible, for example, to use psychoanalytic theory without accepting a Freudian view of gender formation? Who are the analysts to be, and how are we to take account of *their* contribution to the analytic transaction? How shall we come to understand the social dimensions of reading through a mode of analysis so essentially individualized? Moreover, even though it may be important to hold on to the idea of unconscious elements in reading, psychologists are still very far indeed from having provided an adequate or plausible theory of subjectivity and mental processes.

Yet another characterization of the 'common reader' is found in media studies. Much of the analysis of the mass media has been concerned to give a more thorough account of how they communicate with their audiences than is provided either by communications theory or by the simplistic framework of 'balance', 'bias' and 'indoctrination'. Using semiological concepts, media analysis identifies the processes through which a particular chain of associations is encoded and suggests ways in which readers or viewers may be persuaded and guided to decode those messages, producing in the process a range of meanings from dominant through negotiated to oppositional ones. For example, in a study of the television current affairs programme *Nationwide*, Dave Morley focused closely on this range of decoded meanings by interviewing regular viewers of the programme and asking them to talk about their responses to it (Morley 1980). In this case, the questions asked were still intended in part to sustantiate an academic hypothesis – not culpable in itself, but a mode of enquiry we were attempting to move away from. More fruitful, therefore, for our attempt to discover readers' experiences in their own terms was a body of work coming not from any branch of communications studies but from ethnographic sociology, and in particular the work of

Paul Willis and Dorothy Hobson, which starts not with a text or a theory (though it is certainly theoretically informed and alert) but a social group – bikers, schoolboys, housewives – and observes their use of commodities and messages to produce cultures, meanings and interpretations (Willis 1978; Hobson 1980). In a similar fashion it occurred to us that reading might be better understood not by approaching a group of readers with a barrage of predetermined questions and attitudes but by allowing its own account of the place and significance of reading to come to the fore and to define the terms of the study.

At first sight such an 'ethnography of readers' seemed to have enormous potential. Ethnography has an intensely democratic impulse, which provides a useful check against the temptation – strong for socialists, especially academic ones – to speak too readily on other people's behalf, and an acknowledgement of the obvious but easily neglected truth that any account of an activity that ignores or marginalizes the experience and understanding of those directly engaged in it can hardly claim much accuracy or authenticity. Yet ethnography, however enlightened and politically self-conscious, cannot escape the problems affecting all academically based social investigation: how to take account, within the 'neutral' forms and procedures of the analysis, of the immensely powerful and pervasive ideologies that shape all practical language and culture; how and with what authority and on whose behalf to 'interpret' the lives, experiences and meanings of others.

What follows is very far from such an ethnography of reading. It is an attempt, grounded in our theoretical investigations, to break out of the charmed circle of literature and to talk to some women about their reading. Each set of discussions is framed by a particular approach – through schoolteachers, a library, with friends and acquaintances, through group discussion in a women's studies course. What surprised us was the extent to which these 'settings' were more than just a backdrop, how they became actively part of the meaning and significance of the reading we were discussing. In these extracts we highlight the theme of approved and disapproved reading, which came through strongly in all the interviews.

First, a word about the questions. We talked to young women in schools and to women at home, caring for children. The questions we asked were about the women's current reading, about television, newspapers and radio, about memories of reading as a teenager, as a newly-wed, with young children, on retirement; about reading in school, and the pleasures of particular books and authors. With school students, our questions focused in more detail on certain magazines for young women.

We noticed, on listening back to the tapes, how implicated we still are in the academic modes of our training, searching for the single authoritative meaning. Thus on occasion we pressed the women for interpretations of a text by means of questions (What about the ending? What do you think of this character? Is this realistic?) which owe more to the language of teaching and GCE examination than anything else. We had hoped, too, to discover something from the interviews about romance, the staple of women's reading. But in fact what we found to be of more significance and interest to the women we talked to was the 'social conditions' in which reading takes place. Like the well-trained literary critics that we are, we found that we were once more elevating the texts above the social relations and practical circumstances within which they exist and which give them meaning.

Even the small number of interviews that we eventually conducted – seven with young women at school, twelve with women looking after children at home – produced a large amount of material. In the account that follows, we have chosen the words of interviewees throughout to illustrate areas we find interesting and important, and our questions have disappeared.

## Schooling and reading

The young women who talked about their reading attended a large comprehensive school in Birmingham, and were interviewed during school hours. They talked about reading teenage magazines – *Jackie, My Guy, Oh Boy* and *Blue Jeans*. The girls were all in the fourth year, around 15 years old. Eight were in the bottom set, taking CSE English; and six were in the top set and described by their teacher as 'the cream of the cream'. We interviewed the girls in pairs, the girls in the bottom set in four pairs, each consisting of one Asian and one white girl, and the top set in three pairs chosen by the teacher, one of which consisted of an Asian and a white girl, all the others white. They all knew that the discussion would focus on girls' magazines.

Of all the themes that emerged from the discussion it is the sense of approval and disapproval, instituted sometimes by an alliance between home and school, sometimes by conflict between them, that we focus on here. This distance and antagonism between the values of the school and the girls' own views was expressed by two of the top-set girls, who interrupted a discussion about their teacher with the question: 'He's not going to hear what we say, is he?' Since for most of us reading is first learned in school, and English is a school subject, the terms established by school and examination system have a powerful and inescapable influence. Zoe and Trisha from the top set shared with most of their classmates a sense that they shouldn't really be reading the magazines.

> *Zoe.* Once you're doing it you're sort of conscious that it's well, sort of trashy. But you read it 'cos it's silly and 'cos it's there.

Later they talked about their parents' attitudes:

> *Zoe.* Oh they think I waste my time [. . .] think I ought to get on to all these, you know, better books, novels . . . think, oh you're wasting your money.

The top-set teacher echoed this disapproval of the girls' preferred reading: he had 'even found girls in the top set reading them'. Tricia tended to agree that the magazines were a waste of money, but then added laughingly, 'If it isn't very good I find it tempting.'

The disapproval of their chosen reading which all these girls encountered may be more than a question of 'waste of money'. It may also reflect an anxiety that they will 'squander their talents', fail to tend what some sociologists have called their 'cultural capital' – a concept designating the social value that accrues to knowledge associated with and legitimated by the dominant culture, enabling its owner to act with power over those officially designated 'culturally deprived'. For girls in the top set on their way to becoming 'the cream of the cream' and going to university, access to this privilege means conserving their intellectual energy, learning *not* to read and enjoy certain texts, in order to maintain their distance from the majority who do read and enjoy them. The tensions and contradictions in this process were clearly perceived by the two most vociferous of the bottom-set girls, who had also experienced the school's condemnation of the magazines and were defiant about their right to read them.

> *Jane.* You get some of these snobs, you know, they look at the book and they go, 'Oh isn't this disgusting, look at this, isn't it disgusting?' (*Elaine laughs.*) Don't they . . . ?
>
> *Elaine* (*answering our question*). Oh I think they read 'em, don't they? I mean . . .
>
> *Jane.* I mean, perhaps they don't buy 'em, but they look at other people's, you know, and they say 'Oh,' you know, 'dunno what you see in this comic, dunno what you buy it for, it's disgusting.' But there's nothing in there that's too bad.

Being disapproved of is an alluring prospect as well as a repressive one; and the system that divides books and young women into 'good' and 'worthless', 'cream' and 'trash', blossoms at certain moments into an eloquently mute form of insubordination. Asked whether they ever read magazines in school, two of the girls replied:

> *Vicki.* Yes, yesterday. (*Laughter.*) In the English lesson, I had a *Jackie* under the table . . . the school *Jackie*. [. . .] Usually I bring one to school and if I find something's getting a bit of a drag I sort of take it out of my bag and read it for a bit.
>
> *Julie.* In the discussion lessons you tend to do it more 'cos, I don't know, the teacher's rambling away and you don't have to make notes.

Reading under the desk takes its place alongside the other small avoidances and occasional conflicts that make school life bearable for young women. Most teachers in any case, in a mixed school, choose books to satisfy the boys' interests. Reading teenage magazines is like wearing jewellery or making tiny alterations to the school uniform or giggling. It's part of the recognition of the distance and alienation between the ideology of the school system and the practical reality of being a young woman, which includes the reality of a femininity powerfully represented and advocated in the magazines; a recognition, too, that if you're going to 'get on' in the academic hierarchy you will have to accept its terms, and if like the vast majority of women you are not going to get on you will still have to put up with the terms most of the time, even though you never wholeheartedly embrace them. Even for the ambitious and successful top-stream girls, reading is a site of confusion and conflict, because in the process of becoming certificated they will have to learn to be 'one of the boys', and deny much of the condition of womanhood they share with the young women in the CSE streams.[21]

School versions of good and bad reading probably stay with us most of our lives. Women living and working at home remembered the discriminations learnt at school, and still had a strongly internalized sense of the kind of reading which had been disapproved of. The interviews with these housewives took place during the day, while husbands were at work, often with the active participation of babies and young children. Their sense of being 'inferior' readers, in an educational sense, was acutely brought home to us when one woman broke off after a vivid account of a novel to ask: 'Is that all right for your tape?'

The sense of guilt and embarrassment at reading 'trashy' fiction was greatest in a woman who had studied English at A level. That reading she remembered as hard work:

> *Jean.* We read sort of Shakespeare and Milton, you know, the sort of thing you read for A level. [. . .] You just sort of get out of the habit of reading all that heavy stuff, really. You just can't sort of concentrate on it at all. 'Cos, I mean, to read Milton you've got to understand every line, you know, to. . . . It takes you a day to get through a page. [. . .] My family weren't very well educated, you see, so reading's the sort of thing I kept to school, and the sort of things they discussed at school were the books you were doing for exams, you know. But those magazines I used to read when I was twelve or thirteen, I was quite young, I sort of gave up as I got older. I used to get embarrassed by them, to tell you the truth. I used to be embarrassed . . . unless I could read them on my own. I used to think people would make fun of me or something . . . 'cos I read them, you know.

*Maria.* I didn't like them [school books], quite honestly. I think we had books like *Silas Marner* and *Mr Polly*. [. . .] We had a reading list, and I must admit I didn't enjoy the books then. . . . I used to read Agatha Christie books and I started reading the . . . I can never think of the names . . . those *Angelique* books, you know, those . . . but we obviously weren't meant to read those sort of books.

Books we are supposed to read. Books we aren't supposed to read. Books we are bored by. And books we are embarrassed by, not least perhaps because they speak of areas of our experience, our femininity, which we are not supposed to acknowledge or talk about in school. Books which test us for suitability for a job behind a desk, and books which are for ourselves in private, for pleasure and leisure. These distinctions are specific, in the form that they take, to women, though not unique to us. They are quite unacknowledged by the dominant patriarchal discourse, yet its patterns of approval and disapproval clearly affect and may actually structure much of our pleasure in reading, as well as the ideological effects of what we read.

## Families and reading

For the woman who works at home, 'flexible rostering' is a daily reality, and the boundaries between work and pleasure/leisure are constantly changing. Demands on her time can be made by children, husbands, friends, brothers and sisters, at any time of the day or night. She does not clock in or out. She has to *create* time for herself, set her own boundaries, if she can, between working and not working. In our discussions with women in this situation it began to occur to us that reading is a way of creating these boundaries, of clearing a space for oneself.

*Jane.* If I've got a particular book that I sort of like, I'll read it in the evening while they're watching television and things are sort of going on around me. . . . If I'm not working and it's sort of really gripped me I might sort of give them their breakfast and then I'll have a cup of coffee and sort of sit down for half an hour and it might end up that I don't sort of get up till ten o'clock (*laughs*) if it's sort of gripping. If I'm at home I sort of do my work, read half an hour sort of after lunch or something like that till I've finished my book, and then I think, oh, I wish I hadn't finished it so quickly.

Reading alleviates the tedium and isolation of a daily routine which has to be self-imposed; an isolation that can be terminated unpredictably and without warning by others, so that a book you can 'pick up and put down' suits this unpredictability. The demands of housework, and the material conditions in which that work is done, severely limit women's time to read.

*Helen.* I can't read in bed because the baby sleeps there and I can't put the light on.

*Mary.* When I was first married, I never read. I had too much to do. You did more in your house then, baking and bread baking and everything you did . . . your washing . . . and your washing was a blinking whole day with washing and blueing and starching and ironing and damping and there was a lot to do.

As well as the fact that there are certain jobs to be done to keep a household alive and running, and that it is almost always the women in the household who do this work, there is the fact that a woman's time is always available. She is assumed to do nothing all day except read and gossip, and therefore to be at everyone's beck and call when the family is at home. For a woman to claim time for herself by reading in the presence of the family may be a cause of resentment.

*Liz.* My husband used to say 'Put that light off.' He didn't do a lot of reading. He was always too busy.

The same woman recalls her time in service, when the same familial restrictions applied:

*Liz.* When I was in service, I got a very interesting book and I used to go up to my bedroom, and I used to get into bother.

Once again the association between reading and trouble or disapproval – this time not, as in school, the type but the very fact of reading.

*Jean.* He doesn't like me to be reading, so I usually read in the evening before I sleep, take it to bed with me and read it. But he doesn't like me . . . sometimes I might be in the kitchen cooking or something, you know, and if it's interesting I want to get to the end of it, you know. I keep on reading till I've finished it and I take it everywhere and that used to get on his nerves slightly.

'Can't you put that book down?' The irritation a bookworm can cause others is enormous. In some families the irritation derives from a sense that reading is a useless activity, as well as a solitary one: not a practical use of one's time. For a woman to give herself time to read in the company of others is doubly irritating because it means she is claiming time for herself and thus refusing it to other people, something husbands are quite accustomed to do, but a terrible affront to the right ordering of family life when done by a woman.

If reading is a way of 'taking one's time', it is a more effective and satisfying way of doing so than other diversions precisely because of its private character. Several of the women described losing battles with the rest of the family over what to watch on television.

*Maria.* I don't watch anything regularly. I purposely try not to look what's on because I think, oh yes I could . . . I wait until I've got the time and then look, but I mean it doesn't always work out, because my husband looks at the . . . you know . . . the paper, and the children do.

Tensions and arguments of this kind about reading may seem trivial; and yet what they reveal about the importance of privacy, time off, time-wasting and time fought for can, we believe, add an important and neglected dimension to the arguments about cultural politics that we make elsewhere in the book. In the more public struggles over meaning, over the curriculum, over access and publication, this kind of reading, which happens in an unorganized and almost unnoticed way in thousands of homes and workplaces every day, is easily overlooked. An account of these conflicts can remind us that the 'private sphere' of the family is a political and ideological institution too, and that the meanings forged there may be as effectual as those produced in the classroom or the street.

In addition, if women can appropriate time for reading, that reading may lead to wider changes of consciousness. Reading, and talking about reading with other women, can change our perceptions of the world and help us to find the cracks in the walls of patriarchy that surround us.

> *Liz.* Reading educates you. Oh, I think it educates you. If you don't read how can you talk to people? Oh, I think so. Books are nice. I really . . . what I would like . . . to join a reading class, discussion.

It is interesting that Liz is a woman in her seventies who spent much of her life before retirement as an active member of the Co-operative Women's Guild, an organization of the labour movement which has campaigned as vigorously as any for an improvement in the condition of working-class women's lives. As feminists, we make connections between reading and consciousness-raising groups, and between consciousness-raising and political education and change. Although it is material conditions that affect women most directly, it can sometimes be a 'cultural' change which stimulates us to demand something more, and something different. These are large vistas, and the actual connections remain to be made. But they are implicit none the less in the restricted times and spaces, hard-won and disapproved of, in which much women's reading is done.

# 8

# Conclusion, in which nothing is concluded

> The class struggle, which is always present to a historian influenced by Marx, is a fight for the crude and material things without which no refined and spiritual things could exist. Nevertheless, it is not in the form of the spoils which fall to the victor that the latter make their presence felt in the class struggle. They manifest themselves in this struggle as courage, humour, cunning and fortitude. They have retroactive force and will constantly call in question every victory, past and present, of the rulers. . . . A historical materialist must be aware of this most inconspicuous of all transformations.
>
> (Benjamin 1973, p. 256)

'No return to the thirties': the defiant slogan of the Right to Work movement of recent years conceals a paradox; for, in the very act of declaring that the momentum, the 'forward march', of history is and must be irreversible, it acknowledges the ineluctable grip that the thirties continue to exert on the socialist imagination of the present. Outside the realm of kitsch and historical pastiche, of the colour supplements and Mrs Thatcher's neo-Victorianism, no one in the same period has felt any compelling need to escape from, return to or be in any other way more than ordinarily interested in the 1890s, the 1920s or any other available decade. But 'the thirties' – which in this context means mass unemployment, an economy and money system in crisis, a labour movement betrayed by its leaders, fascism in power and the imminence of global war – looks enough like an eerie *Doppelgänger* of the present in its most sinister manifestations to compel both obsessed fascination and defiant repudiation.

Our own argument, too, has made a long circuit, ending where it began with a range of issues – the social origins and public obligations of literature, the role of English in education, the discourse of standards and values, the presence and effect of newer and more popular media – all of which can be seen, as we suggested at the outset, to have received decisive formulation in the years between the wars. For many people on the 'cultural left', Leavis and Richards, as much as their contemporaries Brecht and Lukács, Gramsci and Benjamin, speak still with a relevance as compelling as the morning paper, and as disagreeable.

Of course, the differences, across half a century, are enormous, in culture as in politics, and it is doubtful whether many people under 40 actually *feel* this historical undertow dragging them back towards the thirties. An entire range of terms and concepts, many of them still able to mobilize apparently similar political sentiments, have actually acquired not only new accentuations but a wholly different social content. What does it mean, for example, to call someone who has never had – perhaps never will have – a job, someone to whom 'having a job' has never really become a very meaningful or interesting idea, a 'worker'? In such a case, a sense of exploitation remains, as well as anger and a kind of solidarity. But the specific political and moral sentiments that have been historically convened around the classical relations between capital and labour, the forms of association and action that were developed from them and that constituted the theory, programme and rationale of the *labour* movement and the consolidated *working* class: what can these signify (not nothing, but assuredly not the same either) to the unemployed millions to whom capital can no longer offer even the traditional opportunity to be exploited? And what of the effect of the immensely complicated restructuring of labour itself, in the electronic and cybernetic deskilling of traditional occupations, the internationalization of the labour market, and the intervention of the state as an employer?

The redefinition and rearticulation of political and social

vocabularies has accelerated dramatically in the past five years, the years of Thatcherism or 'authoritarian populism' (Hall and Jacques 1983). Indeed, a consideration of the ways in which the latter differs from and is more than just a euphemism for 'fascism' would bring out many of the important shifts in political meaning since the thirties. But the intrinsic interest and importance of this new Conservatism, and of its European and North American counterparts, should not be allowed to conceal the extent to which the canonical rhetoric and historic iconography of labourism had already been challenged and even superseded well before 1979. This process has exhibited – to quote Benjamin again – both positive and negative moments.

On the negative side, continuities and memories of endurance and struggle, traditions of hard knowledge and experience, were broken, in the years after the war. The occupational and cultural and familial networks, like the actual places that had nourished them, were 'modernized' and 'redeveloped': knocked down, broken apart and relocated. The mental continuities too, with their crucial senses of collective history, identity and reference, have in the same period been poisoned or lobotomized. On the positive side, it is now much more difficult to ignore the extent to which those traditions, and even more the forms in which they have subsequently been represented, spoke only to and for a working class both white and male – 'the lads' – to which those who were neither, as well perhaps as some who were both, could relate themselves only in a subordinate, alienated or antagonistic way. Then those subordinated voices, gathering into new kinds of association and movement, making their own demands in and on the present, begin to find too that they have discovered a history: discovered and created one, since to find a history it is necessary to *rewrite* history, to deliver it of the things it has not yet been allowed to say.[22] This is perhaps that 'most inconspicuous of transformations' of which Benjamin wrote, this calling into question of the past, with a disinclination – humorous, cunning or angry – to defer to the authorized version.

This rewriting of the meanings and narratives of the past is not a one-sided process. The 'Great Power' fantasies that fuelled the Falklands war, the attack on the moral and organization of trade unions; the bizarre but quite conscious and potent collocations of post-industrial technology and 'Victorian' morality, the reinvigorated promotion of standards, canons and traditions in education and cultural life, all involve historical rewritings of a determined and persuasive kind. The question of history, of its meaning for present and future, is now a most urgent political issue. There will be a temptation, under this onslaught, to succumb to a consoling but reactionary conception of 'tradition', and to produce alternative histories of a correspondingly static, simplified and sentimental variety. The practice of cultural politics in these circumstances calls for great delicacy and scruple (Benjamin's humour and cunning), as well as for determination, bloodymindedness and nerve. It is treacherously easy, too, to allow the historical project to become a substitute for confronting the present, a displaced and retrospective utopianism. The declaration that there shall be 'no return to the thirties' oddly mobilizes both responses, a repudiation of old battles, and a powerful nostalgia for them.

Our actual relation to the thirties – to all the ideological constructions and connotations that compose that concept – is both more complex and more intimate. If we wish to lay claim once again to those values of responsibility and self-determination, of 'citizenship', which played such an important part in articulating the public discourses of the thirties, we shall first have to recapture the notion of self-determination from the individualistic Tory philosophy of the 'right to choose' and to inform it, in actual practices and relationships, with a collective social meaning and content which restores to it something of the Jacobin vigour and ruthlessness ('*Citoyens!*') of the original concept, and a sense – usefully reactivated in its Thatcherite appropriation – of social difference and antagonism quite unlike the anodyne classlessness and sexlessness of the thirties 'citizen'. Or again, to come closer to our concerns in this book, many features of the *Scrutiny* enterprise remain exemplary. Its sense of the centrality of reading and writing in the formation of social subjectivities, its open hostility to the literary establishment and the flaccid and self-serving platitudes of literary-critical common sense, its seriously principled bloodymindedness, all these 'belong' to the thirties, while retaining a pertinence which is not diminished, though it is complicated, by the fact that other aspects of *Scrutiny*, its aggressive élitism, its anti-modernism and hatred of popular culture, have themselves become, in suitably sedated versions, the common chitchat of the academies and of their Tory paymasters. What is involved, here, is neither the acceptance of some static historical 'inheritance' nor the simple substitution of a preferred alternative, but a continuous transformation, a 'rewriting', of what we have received in terms of what we have to do.

In this process, not of returning to the thirties, but of acknowledging and understanding our historical connectedness with that time, our own contemporary socialist-feminism has opened up a new set of questions and highlighted the differences between the constructed images and the infinitely more complicated realities of the decade. At the most fundamental level, the received cultural-political image of the thirties as the decade of 'the writer and politics' is sharply disconcerted by the simple recognition that its protagonists, the communist intellectuals, the International Brigade, the Jarrow marchers, the anti-fascists (and the fascists), the Left Book Club subscribers and Orwell's steel-muscled colliers were all *men*. Now, fifteen years after the re-emergence of feminism as a significant movement, it is no longer possible to leave these family snapshots undisturbed, resembling as they do those photographs of the Bolsheviks from which the figure of Trotsky has been carefully eliminated. Were there no women there? None at all?

There were, of course, and the old pictures will have to go. For those images, so powerfully redolent of the connections between 'culture' and 'politics', between 'intellectuals' and the 'working class', are, potentially, an equally powerful reminder of a historical and political *exclusion* – the exclusion of women from the traditional culture of socialism. Perhaps exclusion is not the right word – both too strong and insufficiently precise; because there *are* images of women too, like the women on trade-union banners representing the spirit of democracy or socialism, the women scrubbing the front step and waiting to be freed from the drudgery of housework by modern labour-saving devices, the mothers of children who must be rescued from hunger and want. Images of women are not absent, but they almost never present women actively shaping their future. Rather, women and their children figure as the measure, the symbol, of injustice, and of the progress to be made. They do not march themselves; but it is on their behalf that the marchers do.

Contemporary feminist history has begun to construct another version of Auden's 'low, dishonest decade' – still, of course, a selection and construction, but one whose distance from the received image reveals the existence of complexities which the snapshot memories occlude. In spite of persistent propaganda to the contrary, the women's movement did not die with the achievement of suffrage. Through the twenties and thirties groups of women in direct lineage from the suffrage movement continued to agitate for 'equal citizenship', the most widely supported demand being for equal access to the professions. Campaigning for the 'endowment of motherhood' (family allowances, now child benefit) continued too, as did campaigns for birth control, for abortion law reform, against the sale of prostitutes and both for and against protective employment legislation. There was a strong and diverse women's peace movement, involving a wide range of women from the middle-class Women's International League for Peace and Freedom to the working-class Women's Co-operative Guild. Feminists had a range of formal political affiliations. A few were conservatives, some were communists, some socialists. But the strongest group were the 'radical liberals', with their demand for complete social and political equality between men and women and their insistence on the irrelevance and irrationality of arguments from biological difference. This feminist movement controlled the magazine *Time and Tide* for a period in the twenties and thirties, and counted among its activists and supporters many women writers whose work is known nowadays only because of feminist research and the efforts of feminist publishers.

So there is a third version of women's place in the thirties: not excluded, nor a 'misrepresented presence', but actively organizing together, culturally and politically, alongside men and sometimes against them. Our image of the decade could be of middle-class women like Winifred Holtby and Vera Brittain writing and campaigning and addressing meetings and trying at the same time to make sense of their sexual feelings and their personal lives. Or it could be of the Co-operative Women's Guild wearing *white* poppies on Armistice Day as a symbol of their rejection of militarism and their desire for peace. Or of women campaigning for better post-natal care for mothers and babies, or agitating for jobs and equal pay in the Women's Trade Union League. These are still nothing more than cameos, snapshots, images. There is no sense in which they can fully or even adequately represent that moment of our past and present called 'the thirties'. But they do alert us to two essential lessons to be drawn from that version of history.

First, the counter-hegemonic culture that is the project of socialist cultural politics cannot any more be represented as men's culture/women's nature. Just as it is slowly being recognized that women's political demands are not 'any other business' to be deferred *sine die* to the end of the agenda, but a basic and indispensable component of socialism in the making, so it must be with the politics of culture, of memories, images and meanings. There is important work to be done unpicking the threads that connect culture, politics and activity with men, and nature, suffering and passivity with women, and reinstating images of women's struggles, with their equal or greater power to move and affect us in the present.

Second, because contemporary feminism, like the libertarian movements of the 1960s among which it emerged, has stressed the personal, sexual and affective as much as the legal and economic dimensions of politics, it has become possible, through a revaluation of our history and an unpuritanical appreciation of the opportunities for playfulness and enjoyment made possible by the culture of the 'New Left', to restate the importance of culture – in the sense of songs, poems, plays, films, pictures, music and fiction – to politics itself.

It is not just that political themes of power and control are present in every English lesson, every bookshop, every library. It is also that our choice of symbols and meanings in the political sphere actively promotes or retards our aims. In the thirties Winifred Holtby saw clearly the value to the militant suffragists of their 'mastery of the art of ritual', as well as the capacity of fascism to mobilize its supporters through the use of ritual and symbol (Holtby 1934). It remains true today, as anyone active in the labour movement ought ruefully to acknowledge, that a political activity whose language and imagery connote utter tedium is unlikely to be effective in the creation of a vigorous and popular counter-hegemonic culture – something that a political movement less indifferent or hostile to the power and pleasure of song, rhyme, drama, music and film might have some chance of achieving. How we conduct our demonstrations, rallies, pickets, occupations and meetings matters as much as those activities themselves matter. The immense effectiveness of the 'embrace' of Greenham Base, and the imaginativeness and humour of the 'Save the GLC' campaign, suggest what might be done.

*

Again and again in this book we have returned to question and examine the work of the education system, and have placed the conflicts within it and challenges to it at the heart of cultural politics. Looking back to the thirties, and to even earlier moments of working-class history (the 1890s and 1830s), we have suggested that there are traditions of collective self-determination in working-class education which differ quite markedly from both conservative (selective) and social-democratic (comprehensive) models of schooling. There is real excitement in discovering the tradition of Socialist Sunday Schools, in which the young students ran their own meetings and invited speakers of their own choice, as of the Plebs League and the NCLC, in which the curriculum was explicitly designed to meet the practical needs of the labour movement, with a strong emphasis on Marxist economics and social science, committee work and public speaking.

Neither of these movements placed the study of literature at the heart of their conception of education. The two strands of their educational practice which remain important are, first, their stress on the power of education as a form of self-activity, self-determined and democratically organized, and, secondly, their concern with 'useful knowledge' – not a barren utilitarianism but a partisan appropriation of the political, economic and rhetorical knowledge which they saw as power for working people. It was these working-class institutions, more than any government report, that identified the real value of literature, and that created the conditions for the working-class writing and publishing documented in Chapter 3.

Now, on the other side of *Secondary Schooling for All*, and in the middle of the second great economic depression of the century, it is both easy and very much mistaken to look back nostalgically to those earlier moments and to freeze the complexity of past and present in a sepia-tinted photograph of collier-poets or Jarrow marchers. The reforms in schooling that occurred between 1944 and 1974 – the abolition of the 11-plus exam, the introduction of comprehensive schools, the mounting of arguments against streaming and the traditional curriculum – were passionately supported by women and men who had inherited directly from the pre-war years the belief that education and the knowledge it gave were indeed power, and that 'equality of opportunity' in state-provided schooling would soon erode or subvert the class system in Britain. That their dream has turned to dust, that the reforms themselves were never fully realized, that the new clothes of 'equality' were draped over the old skeleton of privilege and selection – all this is now quite clear to most of the reformers themselves. But it has been clear for much longer to sections of the working-class communities, where alienation particularly from secondary schooling runs very deep. The claim that 'knowledge is power', against a background of graduate unemployment and jobless school-leavers with an armful of GCEs and CSEs, has a very hollow ring.

Yet even now there are strategies emerging, from groups of working-class people whose relationship to school is one of extreme disadvantage and discrimination. For example, Croxteth School in Liverpool, faced with closure by the Liberal-controlled City Council, was occupied by the parents, and education was continued with the help of volunteer teachers and a curriculum decided in discussion between parents, teachers and pupils. In many cities, black people have established 'supplementary schools' to challenge the racism of state education and its incompetence and failure in meeting the needs of black pupils (see Clark 1982). The level of racism in the British school system has now been extensively documented, and the usual official response of providing highly paid advisers on 'multicultural education' has done nothing to reduce it. The response of the supplementary schools movement recalls those earlier working-class initiatives in its collective self-activity, its stress on basic literacy and numeracy and its exploration of 'black studies' – the partisan and useful knowledge of the history, struggles and cultures of black peoples which the white education system has ignored, trivialized or denied.

All this has important connections with the question of literature and English, reminding us as it does of the way in which broader economic, philosophical and political pressures on the direction of schooling help to determine the place in it of stories, poems, plays, speaking and writing. It may be that by relegating the question of 'literature' for the time being, and concentrating instead on the kind of demands that working people make of the education system – 'to speak well and easily and to put things in writing easily' (Schools Council 1968, p. 35) – we may be able to rediscover the hope and belief that 'knowledge is power', and to assist in creating the conditions for a differentiated, accessible and unoppressive 'common culture' in which the writing and reading of stories, poems and plays, as of all other kinds of writing, is neither a privilege nor a burden but simply an ordinary pleasure.

If this process of instating the value of writing, speaking and reading – not as 'life skills' for our allotted places in the labour market but as means to power and control over our whole lives – has started 'outside' the educational apparatus in the supplementary schools, the same connections and emphases must now be taken up inside the schools, and in particular in their English departments. Recall the thirties once again: not this time its working-class movements, but another kind of movement, starting on the fringes of Cambridge colleges, and so impassioned in its evangelism and its conviction of the importance of its message that the agenda of 'literature, criticism, life' that it established still frames public examinations and stocks the book cupboards of secondary schools. Shakespeare, Lawrence, Eliot: all human life, for the top bands of English, is there. Despite the thoroughgoing theoretical 'deconstruction' of liberal-humanist criticism, it remains the most powerful philosophy of English teaching, not because of the coherence or truth of its underlying philosophy and world-view, but because what *Scrutiny* proposed was a practical cultural-educational project, concerned with *what* should be taught and *how* it should be taught, not just in universities but throughout the education system.

That project has not created the conditions for the development of a common culture, for reasons touched on in Chapter 2. But it has never yet been matched by an alternative of equivalent ambition, scope and detail. Feminism and anti-racism have had some impact on the school stock-cupboard, and the issue of 'stereotyping', of the reproduction of racist and patriarchal images and values in fiction, is beginning slowly to be understood. Quite clearly, a 'socialist curriculum' for English teaching cannot be developed and promulgated from the universities and their house journals, as the *Scrutiny* programme has been; and perhaps this helps to explain the ineffectuality of Raymond Williams's solitary attempt to rewrite the Great Tradition with the working class at its centre (Williams 1975, pp. 142–4). But it won't simply emerge spontaneously, either, from the fragmented struggles and initiatives of Croxteth, supplementary schooling, peace studies and feminist teaching. There is a real need to begin to discuss again the principles on which a curriculum designed to help create the conditions for a common culture might be based. A start must be made somewhere, and with a view to promoting such a discussion we suggest that that curriculum will have the following features:

1 It will be democratic in formation and organization, and accountable to the community of people who use it, not with the token accountability of governing bodies and parents' evenings, but through discussion and negotiation around the aims and methods of English teaching.
2 It will be based not solely on reading and criticism, as the major modes of learning and response, but on writing and talking too; and, so far as a pre-existing syllabus goes, it will be studied not in terms of the unique and unrepeatable *production* of 'great literature', but in terms of the centrality and variety of reception as the point of production of meaning.
3 It will aim to create not 'functional literacy' – reading and writing for the labour market – but 'powerful literacy' – the acquisition of those relevant forms of writing and reading and speaking that confer genuine understanding and control, including the extension of speech and writing through the use of tape, video and film.
4 It will subscribe to no Great Tradition, no 'canonization' of

literature. Indeed, it will aim to circumvent the concept of 'literature' altogether, in its bogus opposition to 'language', and replace it with writings, past and present, read as historically formed and informative, and as examples of 'art'. Women's writing, black writing and working-class writings will stand strongly alongside the texts of privileged white men.

5 'Powerful literacy' will open up the awareness and criticism of ideologies, and lead into an understanding of the strength and the construction of images.

6 All this will be assessed only within a framework and according to methods and objectives agreed by discussion between students, teachers and other people involved or interested in the curriculum.

These suggestions can hardly be called utopian. Work of this kind is already being done, piecemeal and marginally, within the existing arrangements. To do it in a more public and organized fashion, across a significant area and to the extent that it challenged the hegemony of the examining boards would be very difficult and would encounter hostility and opposition, some of it understandable. But it seems worth fighting for, and it would be rewarding to try.

*

Among the conclusions to be drawn from the debates about literature, cultural politics and the working class in the twenties and thirties is the great difficulty even on the left of breaking with liberal-humanist discourses of literature and culture, discourses which went unchallenged by large sections of the labour movement and which place literature above politics and ideology, in a privileged sphere of universal truths and values. In a similar fashion, the very widespread association of literature with personal development, supposed once again to be something quite separate from the public domain of politics and economic life, did little to encourage a radical politics of reading and writing. Even those individuals and groups who did perceive the political pertinence of cultural matters were hindered by the lack of organization and communication and received little support, either from fellow-travelling intellectuals or from the labour movement.

The effects of this lack of organization can be seen in the fragmented nature of moves towards a radical literary-cultural politics and the development of working-class writing. In the labour movement there was no general agreement about the need for such a politics. The political parties of the left offered little support either, and where it was forthcoming – as, for example, from the Writers' International and the *Left Review* – it was inevitably limited in scope. There was no centralized organization of cultural-political activity of the kind found, for example, in Weimar Germany, where both the Social Democratic Party and the German Communist Party were directly involved in cultural issues and in the promotion of socialist and working-class writing. In Britain the absence of any such organization, combined with and reinforced by the continued dominance of the liberal-humanist conception of culture, ensured that the audience for working-class writing remained small. Even for those who acknowledged the need for some sort of cultural organization, there was no adequate materialist aesthetic or theoretical understanding of culture and ideology of a kind that would have enabled a widespread evaluation of working-class writing according to norms other than those of the literary-critical establishment.

There were many reasons for this fragmented state of affairs, reasons that highlight the complex sets of relations constraining oppositional and innovative forms of cultural productivity. One reason for the uncoordinated state of cultural politics lay in the political priorities of organized labour, where, not surprisingly, economic and political questions commanded attention and where, when culture and education were considered, it was an education in useful knowledge and skills that was accorded primacy. The failure to address the politics of culture was implicitly supported by the undeveloped state of Marxist theory in this area. In effect, 'culture', as a domain of signs, ideologies and subjectivities, was virtually conceded to the ruling class.

In spite of this, it is remarkable, given the social and cultural character of the inter-war decades, how much was achieved in the field of cultural politics. Those achievements must include the relatively marginalized but still powerfully articulated challenge to the concept of the political neutrality of educational and cultural practices, and the attempts in the Labour College movement to develop alternative practices. Within the rather different constituency addressed by the Writers' International, too, there was some recognition of the central importance of an explicit and organized left-wing politics of culture, ranging from the beginnings of a Marxist theory of literature and culture to the development of alternative forms of writing to supplant mass popular fiction. The inter-war years are also marked by the level and depth of working-class interest in and engagement with education and culture, which led many thousands of women and men to devote their limited leisure to the pursuit of education and the production of writing. The wider recognition of the significance and value of these developments was curtailed by the outbreak of war, in the course of which questions of class were subordinated, at least officially, to popular nationalism.

Looking in more detail at the cultural politics of the inter-war years, we are struck by how much of the thinking and the experience of that period has been subsequently lost for the cultural and educational repertoire of the left. No doubt this is in part because educational and social provision in the post-war period could plausibly represent itself, for a while at least, as having adequately satisfied the demands and agitations of the thirties. State education after the Butler Act soaked up and immobilized many of the more radical alternatives developed before the war. The urge to self-education, too, which is such a striking feature of British working-class culture before 1945, was perhaps diverted to some extent in the fifties and sixties into television, which has also offered an outlet for dramatic representations of working-class life. And of course the cold war and the trauma of the twentieth Congress of the Soviet Communist Party froze, demoralized or drove out all but the hardiest, most dedicated or thick-skinned of the 'generation of '36'. Working-class culture and history has been institutionalized since the 1950s, with the development of social history and the growth of community studies; but this has often been at the cost of neglecting the more radical aspects of the working-class politics of the inter-war years.

Since the Second World War, working-class writers have continued to get their work published, and to write for television and the theatre, on an individual basis, in ways which have tended, in the absence of any interest from the Labour Party or the trade-union movement, to draw them inevitably into the mainstream of bourgeois cultural production. Only in the very recent past have groups been formed, on the basis of class, gender or race, to develop working-class, women's and black people's writing. These groups tend to be based in communities and to publish and distribute their work locally. Many are now affiliated to the Federation of Worker Writers and Community Publishers, which acts as a network for support and information.

The idea and structure of writers' groups has broken with the individualized and isolated nature of much working-class writing before the war. In some respects it resembles developments in the German Democratic Republic since the later fifties, and in the Federal Republic since 1968. As in the earlier period, though, British developments differ from those in Germany in their lack of organized support from political parties or the labour movement.

The common denominator of these groups tends to be locality, gender or race, rather than a shared political or aesthetic position; and the group structure serves to make writing more accessible, and to provide support and critical encouragement. It also helps to get the work distributed and more widely known, and to pioneer new practices of distribution like public readings and local publishing projects.

For all this, black, women and working-class writers are confronted by many of the same problems that faced their predecessors in the twenties and thirties. These include the need to elaborate a popular politics and practical theory of reading and writing, the difficult and continually recurrent issue of form and content, the problem of production and distribution, and the establishment of a ground from which to challenge the dominant cultural and educational norms and practices. The experience of producing alternative forms and methods of writing and reading is in itself an important education for writers and readers, but it also has a broader role to play in the cultural politics of contemporary Britain. And it is here, perhaps, that lessons can be learnt from the experience of the inter-war period. These will include the necessity for a network of intellectual and practical support for writers and writers' organizations; for initiatives to develop an interest in the politics of culture and an established place on the agenda of political institutions like the Labour Party, the TUC, the women's liberation movement and the organizations of black people. It is also clear that an oppositional cultural politics, while needing to develop a broad popular base, must be directed at transforming the dominant practices of education, publishing and broadcasting, which play a central role in maintaining the depoliticization of culture and the marginalization of working-class, women's and black writing. It is here that there is an urgent need for support from people working within the established institutions of education and culture. In this way, perhaps, the hard lessons of the twenties and thirties may yet be persuaded to bear fruit.

*

For the past two years an annual study weekend on working-class writing in the 1930s has been organized by people involved in the Federation of Worker Writers and Community Publishers; and it prompts the question how far the current organization and concerns of working-class writing are consciously or unconsciously modelled on those of the thirties.

The roots of contemporary working-class writing and of the FWWCP are very diverse, and can be traced to locally based community action, changes in the character of adult education, and the example of other similar groups and projects. For many people a knowledge of the history of working-class writing in this century comes *after* rather than before their own involvement. In some working-class households, of course, especially those with a history of political involvement, certain books and authors (Tressell, Jack London and Jack Common as well as Dickens and Hardy) have been read and discussed across several generations. In general, though, it is true to say that most 'worker-writers' in recent years grew up largely unaware of the past records and achievements of working-class cultural activity. Indeed, the British working class, when it did not write and preserve its own history, was systematically deprived of it.

A sense of the past is strong, none the less, in the legitimating of present activities of worker writers, providing a history and serving to refute the notion that writings of this kind (local, anecdotal, autobiographical, non-'literary') are ephemeral, of merely momentary value and interest. It is true, too, that some knowledge of earlier working-class writing has come from the effort to recover, as oral and local history, the lives and experiences of older people.

Discontinuities between the thirties and the present are marked, and on the whole represent an advance. In the thirties, for example, working-class writing was an activity almost exclusively male. Women did write, and even got into print; but the whole institutional basis on which working-class writing was produced and published marginalized the creativity and the experience of women. Today that basis is much more broadly conceived, in terms not only of class but of race and gender. There are, not surprisingly, areas of opposition to these developments, centring on a denial or suspicion of 'sectional' interests within 'the' class. This takes the form less of overt hostility – though both women and gay people have attracted some of that – than of a refusal to recognize that it is possible to organize separately as gays or women while still retaining an overall commitment to the movement as working-class writers. You can be one or the other, but not both; and the irony of white heterosexual men laying down these laws is apparently lost on their most vociferous proponents. In spite of this, we most certainly do not subscribe to the view, apparently current in some sections of the left and the women's liberation movement, that the working class is somehow significantly more racist, sexist or heterosexist than any other class. On the contrary, it has been our experience that, particularly within the Federation, there is a consistently high level of seriousness about, and struggle over, these forms of oppression.

The second major change since the thirties has been in working-class writers' control over the processes of publication. This can be seen in the stress on self-publication and self-distribution, and in the opportunities provided by local writing and publishing projects like Centerprise, Queenspark and Peckham Bookplace. In some cases, a group of writers has selected the contents of an anthology of their own work, typed and illustrated it, printed and collated it, and then sold it themselves. This degree of self-determination is found not just in the publishing but in the actual writing. Members see the workshops as the first audience for their work, and in taking their writing to them they accept and contribute in their turn to a collective process of discussion and revision. Indeed, for many worker-writers, this process forms the basis of their literary development.[23]

Sometimes this preoccupation with writing can seem anachronistic, as if we recognized that we were occupying ground already abandoned in favour of television, video or popular music. Comparisons with the thirties are apposite here too, for already then writing was beginning to feel itself the poor relation of cinema and radio. But the relations between cultural forms are in reality more complex, with the new retaining an intimate relationship and close dependence on the old; and McLuhanite arguments about the obsolescence of writing and reading are unhelpful, particularly when they rest, as they frequently do, on a condescending or contemptuous populism of the kind that supposes that 'real' working-class people don't read – still less write – books, preferring 'the telly'. The fact that the state retains a large stake in the institutions and ideologies of writing and reading should alert us to the continued presence there of major forms of social and cultural power; and the cheapness and durability of printed texts, as well as the great detail and concreteness with which they can still mobilize the imagination, make it unlikely that they will soon lose their usefulness.

*

Contemporary developments in working-class writing and our studies of women's reading and writing testify to the continued importance of fiction in the lives of women and men. We have pointed, in particular, to the expansion of feminist, black and community publishing, but also to the sustained success of popular fiction. If working-class, black and feminist writings are playing a constructive part in current cultural-political struggles, what can be said of popular forms? We have suggested in Chapters 4 and 5 that popular fiction of all types has an important role to play in the reproduction of forms of gendered subjectivity within patriarchy, and that their very power lies in their appeal to and shaping of the real needs and desires of women and men.

From the study of women reading in Chapter 7, it can be seen that reading in itself can function as a moment of oppositional self-determination – at school or in the family, for instance – irrespective of its content. Yet much of the reading pursued by these women against the wishes of those in a position to determine their situation – teachers, husbands, children – is popular fiction, which itself confirms the patriarchal relations of romance and family life. It is, however, worth asking whether there is any evidence of the mobilization of popular forms on behalf of change.

The question of the best form of relationship between men and women and children has been a matter of pressing concern among socialists, anarchists and feminists for many generations, and their 'language of love' has not always been markedly different from that of the despised romantic novelist. The major difference between the two is found not in their account of love itself, nor even in the centrality they accord to it, but in the association between love and marriage. During the early years of the Russian Revolution, Alexandra Kollontai struggled to express and explain the revolutionary attack on the bondage of matrimony while still sustaining a belief in 'the Great Love' between woman and man. And while longing for love, and believing it to be the greatest power on earth, the anarchist Emma Goldman actively dissociated it from marriage:

> Love, the strongest and deepest element in all life, the harbinger of hope, of joy, of ecstasy; love, the defier of all laws, all conventions; love, the freest, the most powerful moulder of human destiny – how can such an all-compelling force be synonymous with that poor little State and Church-begotten weed, marriage?
>
> (Goldman 1931)

The contemporary women's liberation movement in Europe and the USA has once again been embroiled in the question of what to do about marriage, love, sexuality and desire. Campaigns have focused on the laws concerning rape, prostitution, abortion and domestic violence, and on the sexist assumptions of the welfare benefits system. But discussion and negotiation within the movement has been more concerned with desire, celebrating lesbian love with all the force of heterosexual romance, and many of the same codes, while ferociously questioning heterosexual definitions of 'sexual unity', and challenging jealousy, passivity, dependency. The activation of romance on behalf of non-patriarchal modes of female sexuality offers the beginnings of an important challenge to the hegemony of conventional romance in the representation of personal relations.

The impact of these discussions and heartsearchings can be traced in the contemporary genre of feminist confessional fiction, and in particular in the work of Marilyn French and of the British novelist Zoe Fairbairns, who is attempting to develop formulaic 'family saga' fiction from a feminist perspective. Given the breadth and impact of these discussions in recent years, it is surprising and alarming that in so many English lessons romance magazines are still read surreptitiously *under* the desk, and that English teachers 'draw the line' at a serious study of contemporary romantic fiction.

Such a serious study might usefully begin with *The Bleeding Heart* by Marilyn French. French employs the conventions and formulas of romance to explore the problems of patriarchal heterosexuality, bringing out clearly the conflicts basic to the genre and connecting its formulaic elements and procedures directly to feminist questionings:

> And then they were pitched into the middle of a battle, or a battle began inside of them. Chemicals pulsed through thighs and sides, electrical impulses swept through bodies, fingers were charged, lips felt like victims of starvation . . . and they kissed and the war was escalated. . . . Was love always like that, do you suppose? Clamping down on the beloved and crushing them like the bound feet of a Chinese girl-child? How could you work it out, the togetherness, the distance? The old way had been to turn the woman into the man's creature: one will, one mind, one flesh: his. But there was no new way, was there?
>
> (French 1980, p. 23)

*

Here, then, is a field of action for 'English'; but only for an English not so much 'rewritten' as relocated in a continuous activity of rewriting, a process of inconspicuous transformations as fluid, polymorphous yet determinate as history itself. English in this sense can no longer be a 'subject', constituted by a prescribed corpus of knowledge and framed by a dominant point of view. But if that centred and dominative subject is to be deconstructed and its closed and instrumental relationship with the educational apparatus dismantled, then other connections and relations will have to be discovered and consolidated, inside and outside education. We feel this particularly strongly, since the four of us, who when the writing of this book began were all working in the same university and surveying our topic from something like the same privileged vantage-point, are now dispersed across and beyond the terrain of English studies: only one still in a university English department, the other three in modern languages, in youth work, in community publishing and bookselling. Perhaps because we now have rather different relationships to the education system, we would argue all the more strongly that the rewriting of English, its formal disorganization as a school and university subject, will require new forms of organization and connection that cut across and challenge the authority of the boundaries that at present separate subject from subject, reader from writer, teacher from student, and all of us from ourselves.

# Notes

1 For some of the results of this work, see Barker *et al.* (1978) pp. 1–20, and Hall *et al.* (1980) pp. 227–75.
2 For all these terms, see Gramsci (1971).
3 The references are to Matthew Arnold, *Culture and Anarchy* (1869), John Stuart Mill, *Autobiography* (1873) and Henry Sidgwick, 'The Theory of a Classical Education', in F. W. Farrar (ed.), *Essays on Liberal Education* (1867).
4 This is the form in which Lowe's famous remark is usually quoted. What he actually said, in a Commons speech on the passing of the second Reform Bill on 15 July 1867, was: 'I believe it will be absolutely necessary that you should prevail on our future masters to learn their letters'.
5 In *Scrutiny*, 1, 3 (December 1932).
6 The reference is to the harassment of two university English lecturers, David Craig at Lancaster and Colin McCabe at Cambridge.
7 These two London schools – Risinghill for the sixties, William Tyndale for the seventies – have come to symbolize the post-war crisis in education and the highly contradictory nature and situation of 'progressive' schooling. Both were eventually closed down, amid much acrimony between teachers, parents and managers. The full story can be found in Berg (1968) and Gretton and Jackson (1976).
8 Writing by authors from working-class backgrounds goes much further back than the end of the nineteenth century. It emerged with the industrial and agricultural working class itself, in the

context of political, cultural and educational activity. For an overview of early British working-class writing see Mary Ashraf, *Introduction to Working-Class Literature in Great Britain*, 2 vols (Humboldt University, Berlin, GDR, 1979).

9 The widely publicized first All-Union Congress of Soviet Writers, held in August 1934, was an important forum for the formulation of Socialist realist literary theory.

10 The Writers' International was an organization, founded in 1927 and based in Moscow, which had the aim of promoting socialist and working-class writing everywhere.

11 Between 1929 and 1933, the Communist International pursued a policy of 'class against class' which insisted that social democracy was really social fascism, since, like fascism, it was a way of preserving the structures of capitalism by fending off revolution. This policy was succeeded by that of the Popular Front which urged communists, non-Marxist socialists and liberals to unite to defeat fascism.

12 The Mass Observation movement was founded by Tom Harrison, Humphrey Jennings and Charles Madge in 1937. It enlisted many hundreds of ordinary people in sociological research. They were asked to write a report once a month on their daily lives and to write about particular occasions, like Coronation Day. Research was carried out on social attitudes to a wide range of subjects.

13 The immediate impetus for the founding of the WEA came from Albert Mansbridge, a man who had attended University Extension Classes and taught London School Board evening classes. He was committed to the principles of co-operation and of liberal education. From the outset the WEA insisted that education was above politics, encouraging working-class adult education in the interests of citizenship and national ideological unity.

14 Many of the students at Ruskin College were radical trade unionists whose views had been formed by industrial and political struggle and current Marxist thinking. For detailed accounts of the Ruskin College dispute see J. P. Millar, *The Labour College Movement* (NCLC, 1979) and W. A. Craik, *The Central Labour College* (Lawrence and Wishart, 1964).

15 The most influential Marxist texts of the period on the Woman Question were Bebel's *Woman in the Past, Present and Future* (1885) and Engels' *The Origin of the Family, Private Property and the State* (1902).

16 'Letter to Ralegh', in Spenser, *Poetical Works*, Oxford 1912, p. 407.

17 *Scrutiny*, 6, 3 (December 1937), p. 337.

18 The discussion of masculinity is, we realize, extremely tentative, no more than a preliminary skirmish with the issues. We include it, in

spite of this, because we think it worthwhile to state the importance of work in this neglected area and hope that our suggestions may be taken further by others. The most fundamental criticism we would ourselves make of the work at this stage is that while the initial distinction between masculine and feminine romances was helpful in organizing the scope and direction of the study, its continued application has tended to weaken and limit it. Clearly, different kinds of popular writing are, within their social circumstances of production and consumption, accentuated in demonstrably different ways towards identifiable forms of masculinity and femininity. The error lies in supposing that male romance is concerned exclusively with the codes of masculinity (' a man's world') and female romance only with those of femininity ('a woman's place'). We would now frame any study of this kind not in terms of separated ideologies and representations of gender but rather of patriarchal *relations* which in addition to producing particular forms of femininity and masculinity are themselves textually encoded within popular narratives. It follows that our concern would now be with the relations between masculinity and femininity, as they structure and are represented in gendered popular genres.

19 This is available from the Feminist English Group, York University, Heslington, York, or in the Feminist Library, Hungerford House, Victoria Embankment, London, WC1.

20 These events are advertised through WEA networks and in *Spare Rib*.

21 For work on teenage femininity see McRobbie, Angela, in Women's Studies Group (1978) and McRobbie and McCabe (1981).

22 For an account of these developments, see Rowbotham, *et al.* (1979).

23 For a selection of this work, see Federation of Worker Writers and Community Publishers (1978).

# References


Abbs, Peter (1969) *Education for Diversity*. London: Heinemann.

Anderson, Rachel (1974) *The Purple Heartthrobs*. London: Hodder & Stoughton.

Bagley, Desmond (1967) *High Citadel*. London: Fontana.

Bagley, Desmond (1973) *The Freedom Trap*. London: Fontana.

Barclay, Florence (1909) *The Rosary*. New York: Putnam.

Barker, Francis, *et al.* (eds) (1978) *1936: The Sociology of Literature*. Wivenhoe: University of Essex Press.

Barrett, Michele (1982) 'Feminism and the definition of cultural politics'. In Rosalind Brunt and Caroline Rowan (eds) *Feminism, Culture and Politics*. London: Lawrence & Wishart.

Barstow, Stan (1960) *A Kind of Loving*. London: Michael Joseph.

Basch, Françoise (1974) *Relative Creatures*. London: Allen Lane.

Beauman, Nicola (1983) *A Very Great Profession*. London: Virago.

Berg, Leila (1968) *Risinghill: Death of a Comprehensive School*. Harmondsworth: Penguin.

Benjamin, Walter (1973) *Illuminations*. London: Fontana.

Bernikow, Louise (ed.) (1979) *The World Split Open*. London: The Women's Press.

Bernstein, Basil (1971) *Class, Codes and Control*, vol. 1. St Albans: Paladin.

Bernstein, Basil (1975) *Class and Pedagogies: Visible and Invisible*. Paris: OECD.

Bernstein, Basil (1977) *Class, Codes and Control*, vol. 3. London: Routledge & Kegan Paul.

Blythe, Ronald (1972) *Akenfield*. Harmondsworth: Penguin.

Boden, Frederick (1932) *Miner*. London: Dent.

Booth, Wayne (1961) *The Rhetoric of Fiction*. Chicago: Chicago University Press.

Brecht, Bertold (1978) *The Mother*, London: Eyre Methuen.

Brierley, Walter (1935) *Means Test Man*. London: Methuen.

Britton, Ann, and Collin, Marion (1960) *Romantic Fiction: The New Writer's Guide*. London: Boardman.

Bromley, Roger (1978) 'Natural boundaries: the social function of popular fiction', *Red Letters*, 7. London: Communist Party of Great Britain.

Brunt, Rosalind, and Rowan, Caroline (eds) (1982) *Feminism, Culture and Politics*. London: Lawrence & Wishart.

Cartland, Barbara (1942) *The Isthmus Years*. London: Hutchinson.

Cartland, Barbara (1957) *Love, Life and Sex*. London: Herbert Jenkins.

Cartland, Barbara (1965) *Living Together*. London: Frederick Muller.

Cartland, Barbara (1967) *Again This Rapture*. London: Arrow.

Cartland, Barbara (1977) *Vote for Love*. London: Pan.

Cawelti, John G. (1976) *Adventure, Mystery and Romance*. Chicago, Ill.: Chicago University Press.

Cecil, Mirabel (1974) *Heroines in Love 1750 to 1974*. London: Michael Joseph.

Central Advisory Council for Education (1963) *Half our Future*. Newsom Report. London: HMSO.

Cherry, Chris, *et al.* (eds) (1980) *Hens in the Hay*. Edinburgh: Straumullion.

Clark, Jon, *et al.* (eds) (1979) *Culture and Crisis in Britain in the Thirties*. London: Lawrence & Wishart.

Clark, Nel (1982) 'Dachwyng Saturday School'. In Ashok Ohri *et al.* (eds), *Community Work and Racism*. London: Routledge & Kegan Paul.

Colby, Vineta (1974) *Yesterday's Woman*. Princeton, NJ: Princeton University Press.

Cookson, Catherine (1973) *The Mallen Streak*. London: Corgi.

Cookson, Catherine (1974) *The Mallen Litter*. London: Corgi.

Coward, Rosalind (1984) *Female Desire*. London: Paladin.

Davidoff, Leonore (1973) *The Best Circles*. London: Croom Helm.

Dhondy, Farrukh (1974) 'The black explosion in schools', *Race Today* (February).

Drinnon, R., and Drinnon, M. (1975) *'Nowhere at Home': Letters from Alexander Berkmann and Emma Goldman*. New York: Schocken Books.

Eliot, T. S. (1951) *Selected Essays*. London: Faber.

Ellman, Mary (1968) *Talking about Women*. New York: Harcourt Brace.

Engels, Frederick (1902) *The Origin of the Family, Private Property and the State*. London: Kerr.

English, Deirdre, *et al.* (1982) 'Talking sex: a conversation on feminism', *Feminist Review*, 11 (Summer).

Federation of Worker Writers and Community Publishers (1978) *Writing*. London: Federation of Worker Writers and Community Publishers.
Fell, Alison, *et al.* (1978) *Licking the Bed Clean*. London: Teeth Imprints.
Feminist English Group (1982) *Women and Writing*. York: Feminist English Group.
Fleming, Ian (1953) *Casino Royale*, London: Cape.
Fleming, Ian (1959) *Goldfinger*. London: Cape.
Firestone, Shulamith (1972) *The Dialectics of Sex*. St Albans: Paladin.
French, Marilyn (1980) *The Bleeding Heart*. London: Deutsch.
Goldman, Emma (1931) *Love among the Free*. Pamphlet, no imprint.
Gramsci, Antonio (1971) *Selections from the Prison Notebooks*. London: Lawrence & Wishart.
Greenwood, Walter (1933) *Love on the Dole*. London: Cape.
Greenwood, Walter (1934) *His Worship the Mayor*. London: Cape.
Greer, Germaine (1971) *The Female Eunuch*. St Albans: Paladin.
Gretton, John, and Jackson, Mark (1976) *William Tyndale: Collapse of a School or a System*. London: George Allen & Unwin.
Hall, Stuart, and Jacques, Martin (eds) (1983) *The Politics of Thatcherism*. London: Lawrence & Wishart.
Hall, Stuart, *et al.* (eds) (1980) *Culture, Media, Language*. London: Hutchinson.
Heilbrun, Carolyn (1973) *Towards Androgyny*. London: Gollancz.
Heslop, Harold (1929) *The Gate of a Strange Field*. London: Brentano.
Heslop, Harold (1934) *Goaf*. First published Leningrad, 1926. London: Fortune Press.
*The Highway* (1908 onwards) London: Workers' Educational Association.
Hobson, Dorothy (1980) 'Housewives and the mass media'. In Stuart Hall *et al.* (eds), *Culture, Media, Language*. London: Hutchinson.
Holland, Norman (1975) *Five Readers Reading*. New Haven, Conn.: Yale University Press.
Holt, Alex (1977) *Selected Writings of Alexandra Kollontai*. London: Allison & Busby.
Holtby, Winifred (1934) *Women in a Changing Civilisation*. London: John Lane.
Household, Geoffrey (1968) *Rogue Male*. Harmondsworth: Penguin. (First published 1939.)
Howarth, Patrick (1973) *Play Up and Play the Game*. London: Eyre Methuen.
Hoyles, Martin (1977) *The Politics of Literacy*. London: Writers and Readers Publishing Co-operative Society.
Hull, E. M. (1921) *The Sheik*. London: Newnes.
*International Literature* (1932–45) Moscow: International Union of Revolutionary Writers.

James, Henry (1899) 'The Future of the Novel', in Richard Garnett (ed), *The International Library of Famous Literature*. London: Edward Lloyd, Vol. 14.

Jones, Lewis (1937) *Cwmardy*. London: Lawrence & Wishart.

Laski, Marghanita (1981) 'Everywoman', *Quarto*, July 1981.

Lawrence, D. H. (1950) *Selected Essays*. Harmondsworth: Penguin.

Lawrence, D. H. (1929) *Pansies*. London: Martin Secker.

Leavis, F. R. (1948) *The Great Tradition*. London: Chatto & Windus.

Leavis, F. R. (1952) *The Common Pursuit*. London: Chatto & Windus.

Leavis, Q. D. (1932) *Fiction and the Reading Public*. London: Chatto & Windus.

*Left Review* (1934–8) London: Writers' International.

Lehmann, John (1955) *The Whispering Gallery*. London: Longman.

Lewes, G. H. (1850) 'A gentle hint to writing women', *The Leader*, 1. (Under the *nom de plume* 'Vivian'.)

*Literature of World Revolution* (1931) Moscow: International Union of Revolutionary Writers.

Lyall, Gavin (1967) *Shooting Script*. London: Pan.

Macintyre, Stuart (1980) *A Proletarian Science: Marxism in Britain 1917–1933*. Cambridge: Cambridge University Press.

McRobbie, Angela, and McCabe, Trisha (eds) (1981) *Feminism for Girls: An Adventure Story*. London: Routledge & Kegan Paul.

Maitland, Sara (1979) 'Novels are toys not bibles', *Women's Studies International Quarterly*, 2, 2.

Mann, Peter (1969) *The Romantic Novel: A Survey of Reading Habits*. London: Mills & Boon.

Mann, Peter (1974) *A New Survey: The Facts about Romantic Fiction*. London: Mills & Boon.

Mansbridge, Albert (1920) *An Adventure in Working-Class Education*. London: Longman.

Marx, Karl (1973) *Grundrisse*, ed. Martin Nicolaus. Harmondsworth: Penguin.

Mathieson, Margaret (1975) *Preachers of Culture*. London: Allen & Unwin.

Millett, Kate (1972) *Sexual Politics*. Tunbridge Wells: Abacus.

Mitchell, Juliet (1975) *Psychoanalysis and Feminism*. Harmondsworth: Penguin.

Morley, David (1980) *The Nationwide Audience*. London: British Film Institute.

Mulhern, Francis (1979) *The Moment of Scrutiny*. London: New Left Books.

Newbolt, Sir Henry (1921) *The Teaching of English in England* (The Newbolt Report). London: HMSO.

*New Writing* (1936–8) 1 and 2, London: Bodley Head. 3–5, London:

Lawrence & Wishart. New series, 1–3, London: Hogarth Press.

Northwest Women (1980) *Hometruths*. Manchester: Commonword.

Ohri, Ashok, *et al.* (eds) (1982) *Community Work and Racism*. London: Routledge & Kegan Paul.

Oldfield, E. (1983) *Take It or Leave It*. London: Mills & Boon.

Olsen, Tillie (1980) *Silences*. London: The Women's Press.

Palgrave, Francis Turner (ed.) (1861) *The Golden Treasury*. London: Macmillan.

Palmer, D. J. (1965) *The Rise of English Studies*. Oxford: Clarendon Press.

*The Plebs' Magazine* (1909–19), continued as *The Plebs* (1919 onwards) London: Plebs' League/NCLC.

Press, John (ed.) (1963) *The Teaching of English Overseas*. London: Methuen.

Rampton Report (1981) *The Education of Children from Ethnic Minority Groups*. London: HMSO.

Ransom, John Crowe (1968) *The World's Body*. Baton Rouge, La.: Louisiana State University Press. (First published 1934.)

Richards, I. A. (1964) *Practical Criticism* (1929). London: Routledge & Kegan Paul.

Rowbotham, Sheila, *et al.* (1979) *Beyond the Fragments: Feminism and the Making of Socialism*. London: Merlin Press.

Sampson, George (1925) *English for the English*. 2nd edn. Cambridge: Cambridge University Press.

Schools Council (1965) *Working Paper II*. London: HMSO.

Schools Council (1968) *Inquiry*. London: HMSO.

*Scrutiny* (1932–53) Reprinted in 20 vols. Cambridge: Cambridge University Press, 1963.

Showalter, Elaine (1978) *A Literature of Their Own*. London: Virago.

Simmons, S. (1982) *The Tempestuous Lovers*. New York: Dell.

Simon, Sir E. (1936) *Education for Citizenship in Secondary Schools*. London: Association for Education in Citizenship.

Spacks, Patricia Meyer (1976) *The Female Imagination*. London: Allen & Unwin.

Spencer, J. (ed.) (1963) *Language in Africa*. Cambridge: Cambridge University Press.

Spencer, J. (1971) *The English Language in West Africa*. London: Longman.

Swingewood, Alan (1977) *The Myth of Mass Culture*. London: Macmillan.

Tressell, Robert (Robert Noonan) (1965) *The Ragged Trousered Philanthropists* (1914). St Albans: Panther.

Usborne, Richard (1974) *Clubland Heroes*. London: Barrie & Jenkins.

Vološinov, V. (1973) *Marxism and the Philosophy of Language.* First published Leningrad, 1929. New York: Seminar Press.
Worpole, Ken (1983) *Dockers and Detectives.* London: Verso.
Watson, Colin (1971) *Snobbery with Violence.* London: Eyre & Spottiswoode.
Welsh, James (1920) *The Underworld.* London: Herbert Jenkins.
Welsh, James (1924) *The Morlocks.* London: Herbert Jenkins.
Widdowson, Peter (ed.) (1982) *Re-reading English.* London: Methuen.
Williams, Raymond (1975) *The Long Revolution.* Harmondsworth: Penguin.
Williams, Raymond (1977) *Marxism and Literature.* London: Oxford University Press.
Willis, Paul (1978) *Profane Culture.* London: Routledge & Kegan Paul.
Women and Words (1980) *Don't Come Looking Here.* Birmingham: Women and Words.
*Women's Liberation Review* (1972) London.
Women's Studies Group Centre for Contemporary Cultural Studies (1978) *Women Take Issue.* London: Hutchinson.
Woolf, Virginia (1929) *A Room of One's Own.* London: Hogarth Press.
Woolf, Virginia (1947) The Leaning Tower, *The Moment and Other Essays.* London: Hogarth Press.
Wrenn, C. L., and Bullough, G. (eds) (1951) *English Studies Today.* London: Oxford University Press.
*Writing Women* (1981) Newcastle.

# Index


Abbs, Peter, 30–1, 35
Académie Française, 38
Africa, 23–5
*Akenfield*, 21
Alther, Lisa, 133
Althusser, Louis, 2, 109
Ambler, Eric, 81
Anderson, Rachel, 89, 90
Arnold, Matthew, 20, 21, 27, 31, 32, 38, 51, 176
Arts Council, 6
Auden, W. H., 1, 160
Austen, Jane, 25, 28, 107

Bagley, Desmond, 76, 77
Barclay, Florence, 89–91
Barstow, Stan, 118–20
Basch, Françoise, 111
Beauman, Nicola, 111
Bebel, August, 177
Benjamin, Walter, 70, 72, 102, 155, 156, 157, 158
Berg, Leila, 31, 176
Bernstein, Basil, 30, 37, 39
Birmingham University, 1, 3, 122
Bloom, Valerie, 133
Blumenfeld, Simon, 63
Booth, Wayne C., 17
Bradstreet, Anne, 108
Brecht, Bertolt, 7, 37, 156
Brittain, Vera, 160
Bromley, Roger, 80
Brown, Alec, 61
Buchan, John, 73, 79, 80, 81

Caliban, 5, 10
Cambridge University, 19, 25, 26
Cartland, Barbara, 73, 88, 89, 92–100, 102–3
Cawelti, John, 86, 87
Cecil, Mirabel, 89
Centerprise, 171
Centre for Contemporary Cultural Studies, vii, 1, 3
Certificate of Secondary Education (CSE), 35, 39, 118, 147, 150, 163
Ceylon, 23
Christie, Agatha, 73, 151
citizenship, 32–3, 158, 160
Clarke, John, 59
Colby, Vineta, 111
Collins, Wilkie, 73

Comer, Lee Sanders, 139
Common, Jack, 170
Cookson, Catherine, 92, 95, 96–7, 101
Cooperative Women's Guild, 154, 160
Corelli, Marie, 89, 91
Corrie, Joe, 59
Craig, David, 176
Croxteth School, 163
cultural politics, 4, 6–11, 45–6, 166–70
cultural studies, vii, 1, 3, 38

Davidoff, Leonore, 93
Day Lewis, Cecil, 61
Delaney, Shelagh, 120
Dell, Ethel M., 73, 89
Dickens, Charles, 20, 37, 74, 124, 170
discrimination, 25, 28–30, 34–5

Eagleton, Terry, 26
Eliot, George, 24, 38, 71, 115, 151
Eliot, T. S., 38, 66, 73, 164
Ellis, Bob, 58, 59
Ellman, Mary, 110
Engels, Frederick, 177
Englishness, 9–10, 97, 103
ethnography, 145–7

Fairbairns, Zoë, 174
Falklands, 84, 157
fascism, 9, 44, 46, 61, 79, 156, 157, 159, 161, 177
Federation of Worker Writers and Community Publishers (FWWCP), 133, 135, 138, 169, 170–2, 178
feminist criticism, 26, 107–28 *passim*, 140–4
Feminist English Group, 123, 178
Firestone, Shulamith, 88
Flaubert, Gustave, 16
Fleming, Ian, 74, 75, 76, 84
Forsyth, Frederick, 84
French, Marilyn, 133, 174

General Certificate of Education (GCE), 25, 30, 40, 118, 142, 147, 150
Glyn, Elinor, 89, 91
*Golden Treasury, The*, 19, 37
Goldman, Emma, 173
Gramsci, Antonio, 9, 53, 72, 79, 156
Greene, Graham, 1, 81
Greenwood, Walter, 64
Greer, Germaine, 86, 88

Hadow Report, 31, 33
Hall, Stuart, 157, 176
Hanley, James, 63, 64, 66
Hardy, Thomas, 29, 170
Harrison, Tom, 47, 177
Heilbrun, Carolyn, 110
Heslop, Harold, 56, 58–9
*Highway, The*, 45, 48–51
Hines, Barry, 38, 118
Hoare, Quintin, 30
Hobson, Dorothy, 146
Hoggart, Richard, 3
Holbrook, David, 35
Holland, Norman, 144–5
Holtby, Winifred, 160, 161
Hope Waddell, 23
Horner, Arthur, 42
Household, Geoffrey, 79, 80–5
Howarth, Patrick, 79
Hoyles, Martin, 30, 36
Hull, E. M., 89, 90–1
Huxley, Thomas, 21

India, 14, 23–4
Isherwood, Christopher, 1

Jacques, Martin, 157

James, Henry, 15–18, 31, 124
Jennings, Humphrey, 177
Jones, Lewis, 42, 63

Khartoum University, 24
Kipling, Rudyard, 21
Knights, L. C., 32
Kollontai, Alexandra, 173

Laski, Marghanita, 128, 130
Lawrence, D. H., 1, 13, 14, 74, 75, 114, 164
Leavis, F. R., 17, 22, 24, 28, 31, 32, 33, 35, 156, 164
Leavis, Q. D., 17, 71, 73, 164
Le Carré, John, 73, 81
Left Book Club, 60, 159
*Left Review*, 45, 46, 47, 60–5, 66, 68, 167
Lehmann, John, 45, 65–6
Lewes, G. H., 128
Lindsay, David, 25–6, 32
literacy, 13–15, 16, 17, 20, 21, 36–8, 165–6
*Literature of World Revolution*, 45, 58–9
London, Jack, 170
Lowe, Robert, 22, 176
Lukács, Georg, 55, 156
Lunacharsky, Anatoly, 55
Lyall, Gavin, 77

McCabe, Colin, 176
McLuhan, Marshall, 172
McRobbie, Angela, 178
Madge, Charles, 47, 177
Mailer, Norman, 75, 114
Maitland, Sara, 133, 138–9
Mann, Peter, 144
Marx, Karl, 79, 155
Marxism, 3, 22, 26, 42, 46, 51, 53–4, 62, 66–9, 109, 111, 124, 127, 162, 177
Marxist-Feminist Literature Collective, 123, 167–8, 177
masculinity, 71, 73–9, 80, 82, 84–5, 109, 119, 177–8
Mass Observation, 47, 177
Mill, John Stuart, 20, 176
Miller, Henry, 75, 114
Millett, Kate, 75, 110, 112, 113–14, 115
Mills and Boon, 88, 91, 144
Milton, John, 14, 25, 29, 30, 71, 150
Mitchell, Juliet, 102, 143
Morley, David, 145
Morley, John, 22
Mudie's Circulating Library, 89
multiculturalism, 35–6, 163

National Council of Labour Colleges (NCLC), 48, 52–8, 162, 167–8, 177
*Nationwide*, 145
*New Writing*, 45, 47, 65–6
Newbolt Report, 19, 20, 22, 25, 31, 32, 38, 54, 55
Newsom Report, 33–4
Nichols, Grace, 133

Olsen, Tillie, 106, 136, 139
Onlywomen Press, 109, 131
Orbach, Susie, 133
Orwell, George, 1, 2, 33, 47, 159
Ouida, 89
*Outwrite*, 109
Oxford University, 19

Palgrave, F. T., 19, 37
Peckham Bookplace, 171
Perren, G. E., 24
*Plebs, The*, 45, 46, 48, 51, 52–8, 64, 68, 162
Plowden Report, 35
Pope, Alexander, 14, 16
psychoanalysis, 144–5

Queenspark, 171

racism, 9, 10, 14, 44, 90, 98, 163–4, 171
Ransom, John Crowe, 17
reading, 140–54 *passim*, 165
Richards, I. A., 24, 34, 156
Rider Haggard, H., 72, 73
Risinghill School, 39, 176
Robbins, Denise, 89, 91–2
romance, 71–4, 75–6, 86–105 *passim*, 144, 147, 149, 151, 173–4
Rowbotham, Sheila, 178
Ruskin College, 52, 177

Salinger, J. D., 118
Sampson, George, 22
Sayers, Dorothy L., 71, 73
Schools Council, 34–5, 36, 164
*Scrutiny*, 17, 22, 32–3, 38, 62, 158–9, 164, 165, 176, 177
Searle, Chris, 31
Shakespeare, William, 5, 25, 30, 36, 74, 142, 150, 164
Sheba, 131
Shelley, P. B., 24, 37
Showalter, Elaine, 111, 116
Sidgwick, Henry, 20, 176
Sidney, Sir Philip, 71
Simon, Sir Ernest, 32
Sinclair, Upton, 56
Snee, Carole, 26
Spacks, Patricia M., 111
*Spare Rib*, 109–10, 131–2, 178
Spens Report, 33
Spenser, Edmund, 71, 177
*Spinster*, 133
Straumullion, 131
supplementary schools, 163–4
Tawney, R. H., 32
Tennyson, Alfred, 18, 24, 37
*Time and Tide*, 160
Toller, Ernst, 56
Tressell, Robert, 57, 170
Trotsky, Leon, 22, 55, 159

Usborne, Richard, 79

Virago, 130–1
Vološinov, Valentin, 5

Watson, Colin, 79, 84
Welsh, James, 56, 59
Widdowson, Peter, 11
William Tyndale School, 39, 176
Williams, Raymond, 3, 26, 129, 165
Williams-Ellis, Amabel, 63
Willis, Paul, 145
*Women and Words*, 136
Women's International League for Peace and Freedom, 160
Women's Liberation Movement, 7–8, 9, 86, 88, 107–39 *passim*, 143–4, 154, 171, 173–4
*Women's Liberation Review*, 132–3, 139
Women's Press, The, 131
Women's Trade Union League, 161
women's writing, 128–39 *passim*
Woolf, Virginia, 115, 134
Workers' Educational Association (WEA), 45, 47, 48–51, 52, 53, 126, 132, 177, 178
Worpole, Ken, 44
Writers' International, 45, 46, 58–61, 167, 177
*Writing Women*, 132, 133

Yonge, Charlotte M., 89
York University, 123, 178